Shopping

Shopping

Social and Cultural Perspectives

JENNY SHAW

polity

The right of Jenny Shaw to be identified as Author of this Work has been asserted in accordance with the UK Copyright, Designs and Patents Act 1988.

First published in 2010 by Polity Press

Polity Press
65 Bridge Street
Cambridge CB2 1UR, UK

Polity Press
350 Main Street
Malden, MA 02148, USA

ISBN-13: 978−0−7456−3861−4 (hardback)
ISBN-13: 978−0−7456−3862−1(paperback)

A catalogue record for this book is available from the British Library.

Typeset in 11 on 13 pt Bembo by
Servis Filmsetting Limited, Stockport, Cheshire.
Printed and bound by MPG Books Group, UK

The publisher has used its best endeavours to ensure that the URLs for external websites referred to in this book are correct and active at the time of going to press. However, the publisher has no responsibility for the websites and can make no guarantee that a site will remain live or that the content is or will remain appropriate.

Every effort has been made to trace all copyright holders, but if any have been inadvertently overlooked the publisher will be pleased to include any necessary credits in any subsequent reprint or edition.

For further information on Polity, visit our website: www.politybooks.com

Contents

Acknowledgements

The idea of a 'single authored' book is always a fanciful one, and to claim such in this case would be outrageous. In addition to the patience and forbearance of all those at Polity who have worked on the book with me, especially Jonathan Skerrett, and the kindness of unknown reviewers, there is a legion of friends. Shopping is a central part of relationships with friends and family, and discussing shopping, or sharing the doing of it, with Jennie Bamford, Betty Mechen, Margaret Boushel, Carol Dyhouse, Jenny Harris, Susan Joekes, Niki Khan, Jill Lewis, Liz Mestheneos, Marcia Pointon, Carole Satyamurti and Anna Walnycki, has been critical. I thank them all, heartily. I am especially indebted to my colleague Janice Winship with whom I once embarked on a study of Marks and Spencer and its 'cultural success', but which, as history overtook both the store and us, came to seem ill timed, if not misleading. That study, however, continues to inform my thinking about shopping. Ann Marcus gave me wise and judicious counsel, and the space and time in New York and Maine to write a good part of the book, while Robert Cassen, George Irvin and Fiona Wilson read and commented on separate chapters. My deepest thanks go to Elaine Sharland, Andy Smith and Barbara Lloyd, three guardian angels, without whose wisdom, wit, patience, intellectual generosity and encouragement I could not have completed this book, and to George, Ann and Geraldine Wilkinson, for their love and humour, as well as technical support. All too easily we overlook what is important because we take it for granted. This is true both of shopping and family life, and setting me on the path to thinking seriously about shopping were my mother, Edna Shaw, and her sister, my aunt, Ethel Mann.

1

Shopping in the Rain

'Why do we go shopping?' It seems such a simple question and the most obvious answer, 'to buy the things we need or want', equally so. But after a moment's thought most of us can remember times when we entered shops and did not buy, or even intend to buy. There are many reasons for shopping, or for thinking about shopping, however we choose to do it, yet, if asked to explain ourselves, we can be taken aback. Or, at least I was when, after returning from a walk and talking to a friend about how I had gone into a shop, she asked 'Why?', and I replied 'Because it rained.' Though true, it seemed an inadequate answer. We could have gone on to discuss whether some intention or motive is needed to explain shopping, or whether because, as a species, we humans are very responsive to our environments, my running for cover in a dress shop in lower Manhattan was only to be expected, but we let the matter drop. The next day, at passport control in the UK, I was asked, 'Where have you come from today?', and I answered, 'New York'. The official then asked, 'Working, or shopping?' to which I replied 'Both'. Then, I asked him, very politely, 'Would you ask this of a man?' He did not reply, so I pressed, 'Would you?', and then he shook his head. Perhaps I should have let that go too. Only a few hours earlier, the friendly check-in staff at

JFK, amused by the number of books on shopping buried among my clothes, as I hauled them out to reduce the weight of the bag, wanted to know why I had those books. Then, after I told them, they wanted to know why was I writing another one?

In his book *'Why'*, Charles Tilly (2006) argues that there are four types of reasons which we give for what we do: 'conventions', which are the most culturally acceptable reasons; 'stories', which show a clear cause and effect; 'codes', which govern action, often legal; and specialist 'technical accounts'; and that in every instance, when we give, ask for, or consider a reason, we negotiate a relationship. To my friend, I perhaps gave a technical reason; to the official at Heathrow I gave a conventional reason; and at JFK I gave a story. It started, as does this book, with time and space. With Jonathan Gershuny's (2000) finding that in the rich nations, such as Britain and the United States, shopping is the daily activity on which, after work and sleep, we spend most time, and with Will Hutton's (2002) revelation that in Britain retail footage had expanded to over five times the European average. A figure possibly much larger now, and one reflected in the fact that shopping regularly tops the list as Britons' favourite leisure activity. We spend the time we do shopping not because shortages force us to queue for hours on end, or because we are compulsively acquisitive, but because, in addition to shopping being the mundane reality of buying the things we need to live and, more importantly, do not, and cannot, make for ourselves, shopping makes our lives more meaningful because it is both more and less than buying.

As an activity which straddles the boundaries between work and leisure, production and consumption, pleasure and duty, shopping can be hard to pin down. But shopping is more than buying because of the different ways in which it can be done, the different effects which it can have on the shopper, on staff in a shop or a call centre, on other customers, and those for whom the shopping might be done. However, shopping is also less than buying because it often does not result in a purchase, and sometimes was never intended to. A 'good' shopping trip can be one where money is 'saved' by not buying, just as much as one which does. Even shoplifting, which is a measure of desirability, is shopping, and so is 'window shopping', especially at night when the shops are shut.

Shopping may be mundane, but it is also both an expression and a reflection of culture, which means that we can learn more about culture by looking at shopping. Of course, this is true, too, of much else and, as shopping is seen by many people as a total waste of time it might seem an odd choice of lens. However, no activity is without meaning, which makes the question more whether we can see the meaning of what we are doing when we go shopping?

We are usually 'blind' to our own culture, our 'way of doing things', because it is part of us, in much the same way as we cannot hear our own accents, we cannot, unless brought up short, see our own culture which is the collection of values, beliefs and practices which define our society, which help us make sense of our lives and hopes, and which hold us together both as individuals and as a community. It is a huge job, for culture, a national culture, or more specifically a class, gender, age or ethnic culture to achieve all this, and it has be incorporated, or internalized, and taken for granted. Thus any sample of culture which we might choose to use to shed light on the concept, had better have this feature, and shopping does. Those of us lucky enough to live in a rich settled society so take shopping for granted that often we cannot accurately remember the last time we did it, or what we bought. When teaching about these matters, I would sometimes ask students about the last time they went shopping, which on the whole did not spring to mind, and to list all the shops in a street which they thought they knew well, and then walk along it and check. Most found that they had 'missed' at least a third of the shops, that there were several which they had never noticed before, and some businesses, for example, the insurance company, nail bar, estate agent, funeral parlour, poodle parlour, barber shop and Indian take-away, which they were unsure if they counted as shops.

Within us and without us

Culture is both inside and outside us, and while we may not notice our own culture we might notice its effects on others, and almost certainly on ourselves when we are in another culture. For

Japanese tourists in Paris, the shock at how they were treated by shop assistants there was apparently so acute that every year some have needed treatment for a type of depression known as 'Paris Syndrome', and to be repatriated. In contrast to Japan, where 'the customer is king', it seemed to the Japanese that in Paris the shop assistants barely looked at them. Yet, for many Britons, what shocks them when shopping in France is being chastised for showing irritation at a slow-moving queue because the assistant is firm in giving full attention to the person they are serving at that moment. Shopping is not the same everywhere because the meanings it carries are not the same everywhere, and there is a sense of shopping as a national flag, an advertisement for perhaps both local and national culture: so tourists, like the Japanese in Paris, flock to local shopping areas to sample it. However, in a globalized world, tourists are often disappointed to discover that the local crafts on sale turn out to have been 'made in China'. Shopping reflects the global culture every bit as much as it does the local culture. As Alan Ryan (1998) notes, there is a widespread fear that mass culture will destroy culture, in Matthew Arnold's version of culture as 'the best' and what a 'cultivated person' will appreciate, and, instead, impose a bland uniformity across the world depicted through the image of its becoming 'one vast suburb, filled with indistinguishable shopping malls supplying designer jeans and fast food'.

This is not presented as a pretty sight, and I am not endorsing it, but using it to make the point that the globalization of industrialized capitalism has transformed the geography of production and consumption and led to the nations where consumption is concentrated, for example, Britain and the United States, to become increasingly 'retailized'. As a result, in those nations, it is now easier to find a sign to a mall or shopping centre than to a mine or manufacturing facility, there are more jobs in stores, marketing and advertising than in factories, and more shops are added, almost daily, to museums, hospitals and airports. These are also nations where, to further raise footfall, more cinemas, ice rinks and, in Portugal, even a bull ring, have been added to malls, and where retail 'parks' pepper the countryside as much as the cities; and where every other page of even serious newspapers such as

The New York Times advertise some special shopping deal, while in their cities it is not falling leaves that mark a changing of the season, but changing displays in shop windows. The city, which has long been the most powerful emblem of modern society, remains so, but it is no longer work in a city which is the template modern experience, but shopping in one. This retailization of culture, and an increasing government expectation that the experience of shopping in the population at large will equip it to cope with all manner of 'privatizations', has placed shopping at the centre of 'the way of life of a whole people', a definition of culture which, for Raymond Williams (1958), was the only way in which that could be understood.

Retailization is an aspect of the post-industrial society. Period. However to hear some say of shopping that is has become 'a way of life' is not to hear it as neutral statement, but a criticism of some person or community who is deemed to be interested in nothing but accumulating mountains of goods and gizmos, at the expense of a much richer personal, political and cultural life, which could be theirs, if only they would give up their pathological, selfish and irresponsible addiction to shopping. This view of shopping as a symbol of all that is wrong with the modern world, and as indistinguishable from 'consumerism', is a major obstacle in the attempt to take shopping seriously. But 'retailization' is not the same as the 'consumer culture' or 'consumerism' and this book is not about either of those, or about any of the goods which we buy, or might buy, but about the social and cultural meaning of shopping, as an activity. Retailization may have made or be on the way to making shopping 'a way of life', but shopping is not how most of us spend most of our money, unless we are teenagers of moderately well-off parents still living at home. After taxes, most personal expenditure goes on housing, utilities, transport, insurance, health, education, holidays and various services, whether these mean haircuts, dry cleaning, taxis, eating out, or some form of entertainment. What remains to be spent as 'shopping', whether in shops or online, is mostly not spent on unnecessary luxuries, unless food, clothes, toiletries, cleaning materials and electrical goods count as such. The point is that everyone, except The Queen, goes shopping, even if they do not all shop in the same shops or have the same amount of money to spend. This makes shopping a mainstay of the common culture, even the global common culture, because it can be, and often is, done without a shared language, and as a mainstay of *everyday* life. This is where the story must start.

Extraordinary everyday life

When in Britain a campaign called History Matters (2006) was launched to raise awareness of history and the place of everyday life within it, and provide a time capsule for posterity, it started by inviting the whole nation to write a weblog for one day in October. The response was almost overwhelming, though, for many commentators, also deeply disappointing, as it was full of accounts such as, 'I got up, ate breakfast, and went shopping.' However this is exactly what posterity needs to know, as do we, and the rest of this book can be read as a deconstruction of that sentence. We need, and take comfort from our habits and routines, even though they can be boring, because they bring meaning into our individual lives by providing stability, structure, and representing normality. Indeed, the words 'normal', 'ordinary' and 'everyday' are almost interchangeable, as for many people what they think of as 'everyday life' is what they, as 'ordinary' people, 'normally' do. This is why after 9/11, Mayor Giuliani of New York counselled his fellow American citizens to keep on shopping. At first, this seemed grossly inappropriate, but it made sense because shopping is normalizing, keeps up spirits, and may have helped head off an economic downturn. This is also why after some earthquake or hurricane, a bombing in Kabul or Baghdad, stories about life returning to normal are pictured as people going about their daily lives, shopping. Routine anchors us, and gives us some purchase on the day. Once we have become accustomed, say, to cleaning our teeth twice a day, morning and night, if for some reason we cannot do this, we can feel 'put out' for the rest of the day. Getting back into a routine means being able to take things for granted and go about our everyday lives without worrying too much. Similarly, though we often take vacations to get away from routine, including routine shopping, these very routines are often immediately recreated on holiday. Not because we have nothing better to do, but because shopping bridges home and away, and much of the shopping done while on vacation is for presents to take home and give to those who were left behind. It keeps us in touch with normal life, as we are all traders.

Though culture is about drawing distinctions and boundaries it is also profoundly ordinary and, while Raymond Williams (1976) is famous for having nominated culture to be the most complicated word in the English language, he also described it as plain ordinary (Williams, 1958). In my view this is the most useful aspect of culture to keep in mind when thinking about shopping. That said, shopping means many different things to different people, and at different times. Shopping with some money in your pocket, is very different from shopping without, and there is for most people both 'special' shopping and ordinary shopping. However even the ordinary can become extraordinary and a shop which, to one person, is totally devoid of all meaning or creative potential, is to another person full of opportunity. In Ann Patchett's (1998) lyrical novel *The Magician's Assistant*, a resident of Nebraska gently explains to her new-found sister-in-law the joys of Wal-Mart, 'I bring the boys here in the dead of winter when the weather is awful and they are bored, and I come here when I want to be alone. My mother and I come here when we want to talk privately, and Bertie and I come here when we feel like seeing people. I come here when the air conditioner goes out in the summer and I buy popcorn and just walk around. Most of the times I can remember that when Howard and I were actually getting along he'd ask me if I want to go to Wal-Mart with him, and we'd look at stuff we wanted to buy and talk about it – wouldn't it be nice to have a Cusinart, wouldn't it be nice to have a sixty-four piece sprocket set. It's a very romantic place, really.' This is the point, shopping is not all the same, or always the same.

For many men 'shopping' means 'shopping for clothes' and in their mind, perhaps, equates to 'non-essentials' so that, hand on heart, some men claim that they never 'go shopping', though what I suspect this usually means is that they do not like shopping for clothes, so do it as infrequently as possible. To get a sense of how discriminating people are about shopping, invite someone to talk about their shopping, and if they are not immediately alarmed and defensive, they will cagily ask 'What sort of shopping?', 'food shopping', 'clothes shopping', 'Christmas shopping', shopping alone, shopping with my partner, with a friend, or with the kids? Even if they settle on a category, say, household or food shopping, further clarification, for example, between 'weekly' and 'top-up' shopping is likely to be required. Sorting like from unlike, or classifying, is the basis of all culture, and systems of meaning, and recognizing how carefully we distinguish or discriminate different types of shopping is step one in understanding why shopping is important as culture. However, people are not only discerning about shopping, shopping means being discerning and it is because of the scope which shopping offers to make choices that it can be humanizing.

Thomas Hine (2002:19) writes, 'The local Wal-Mart is the wonder of the world. Never before have so many goods come together from so many places at such low cost. And never before have so many people been able to buy so many things.' The 'buyosphere', Hine's term for all the different places and ways of buying, in the richer parts of the world, is a fulfilment of an 'ancient dream of plenty for all', and has become the 'chief arena of expression' and 'the place where we learn most about who we are, both as a people, and as individuals'. Too much choice, and it can be overwhelming, but even the poorest of us in the rich countries are discerning shoppers, and denying individuals the choices which shopping offers is tantamount, in the modern world, to denying them a right of citizenship. Shopping can be enriching and meaningful, but it can also be boring and oppressive, a feature which, in addition to taking for granted, it shares with the context in which most of it occurs: everyday life.

Poachers and gamekeepers: rules and close shaves

In their book on this topic, titled *Escape Attempts*, Stanley Cohen and Laurie Taylor (1976) start by describing everyday life as an 'open prison', though they soon turn to the various 'fantasies', 'free areas' and 'activity enclaves' which bring relief to the 'mind-deadening' aspects of that 'prison'. Cohen and Taylor do not include shopping as an example of these, though for many women this is exactly what shopping provides: an escape from the family and a bit of time for themselves or to share with a good friend and even, perhaps, recover their more creative side. Another theorist of everyday life, Michel de Certeau (1988), approached the topic through the opportunities which it offers for 'tactical resistance', for being subversive, and finding uses for things and places other than that or those for which they were intended, and which he calls 'poaching'. Many of the uses we make of shops count as 'poaching'; 'shoplifting' is the most obvious example, but we are also poaching when we use shops as somewhere to wait for a friend and yet look purposeful, as a place to sit down in, or shelter from the rain, or to warm up, or as a short cut or, most commonly, for the use of a bathroom. Even more daring, though, is the example given by an ex-IRA man in a radio talk, which included a description of how to 'lose a tail'. The best method, he claimed, was to find an old-fashioned department store, as their layouts were usually so complex that no one but a local could ever or easily find the exit. He then described how, on one occasion, while living in Birmingham, once he realized that he was being followed, he had leapt on a train to Leeds because there he knew of a store where he could be sure of losing his pursuer. When IKEA opened a store in Red Hook, New York, and provided a free water taxi service to it from Manhattan, it was inevitable that the service would soon be used by more than those planning to shop at IKEA, that is, 'poached', and just as inevitable that IKEA would find a way to identify and filter the two groups.

A more ordinary escape offered by shopping might be the switching from one chore to another so, while I might not need, right now, to go and buy toilet paper or catfood, if I choose to do so it is very often because it allows me to escape some other chore, and is satisfying because it gives me a small sense of control over my time. As a break, it punctuates the day and, just as punctuation gives meaning to a string of words by breaking it up, so breaking up the day, which shopping allows, gives meaning to the flow of experience. The shopping break, not only gives structure, pattern and meaning to the day, it does it for the week, the month, and even the year as Christmas shopping comes round once more in October. The tension between 'structure' and 'agency', or 'social coercion' and 'individual freedom' which accords to individuals a degree of control over the shape of their life, and makes them actors, not puppets, is the problem at the heart of sociology. A problem which is never resolvable, and nor do we want it to be, for we want both structure and agency. We want to be able to assume that buses and trains will run on time, garbage be collected, and schools open when the kids get there. And shops too, so that we can use them on the way back, partly because this gives us more room to manoeuvre, but also because if shops are shut unexpectedly, buses and trains cancelled or late running, it undermines everything else. This tension between the sense of freedom, and of being governed by routine is acted out many times every day, as rules and routines are both observed and flouted in shopping, as in other activities. The sudden remembering of an item which 'has to be bought' can be demanding and oppressive, but it can also be liberating, as it is when we spot something we fancy, question whether we can afford it, and then go ahead and buy it anyway.

For philosopher Peter Winch (1958) it was only because human beings are interpretive rule-and-routine following creatures that the systematic study of social behaviour, that is, social science, was ever a possibility. Rules and routines do not determine our behaviour, but they guide it, as is indicated by the phrase 'as a rule'. We need rules because we need and desire structure, stability and predictability in order to get on with our lives, and so deep is this need, that we quickly invent rules when need be. And when we break a rule, we usually invoke another one to justify that breach. Kate Fox (2004) illustrates this in her account of English life as rule-ridden when she adds to the rule identified by Daniel Miller (1998) of 'shopping as saving', which means spending money now in order to spend less later, the rule of 'apologizing and moaning', which kicks in after someone has paid the full price for some expensive item. But rather than keep quiet about this, Fox further observes, the English either blame themselves by saying 'Of course, I shouldn't have . . .', or blame the shop, 'Ridiculous price. . .'.

But to this, we might add, with the secret satisfaction, nonetheless, of having introduced the price into the conversation.

A structure made of rules, or routines, is always provisional and the 'right' of the individual to duck a rule, or change their routine, is treasured every bit as much as the fact that rules are mostly followed. Many times every day we have to decide whether to do something 'properly' or cut a corner, a decision to follow or flout a rule, which illustrates how the everyday world is a moving interface between the order of the society and the pragmatism of the individual. The rules of shopping, such as which side of the counter to queue, are not codified like the rules of the road (except for laws forbidding the sale of alcohol and cigarettes to the under age, sometimes posted inside a shop), so we cannot google them, yet keeping them is something we absorb and follow without realizing it. Other shopping rules we make for ourselves: for example the order in which we go round the supermarket, how we pack our bags at the checkout, and whether or not we tie the handles of the plastic bags together to ensure that items do not fall out in the boot of the car (do women do this, or is it just men?). These are rules to which we may become so deeply attached that we often resent and reject offers of help from others, unless they agree to follow them too and pack the bags our way.

Many of the rules structuring everyday life, such as facing the person you are talking to or keeping 'the right distance' from another person, are what Thomas Scheff (1984) called 'residual rules', ones which only come to light when broken. Though what is the 'right distance' varies according to context and culture as when standing close to another person in a crowded shop is acceptable because it is unavoidable, it is not acceptable when that shop is not crowded. A shop queue is a rule, the making of a line, and it is one which, if broken, will reliably provoke a sharp reprimand from another shopper who will show irritation, and publicly shame the 'offender' by indicating to other shoppers that an attempt to queue-jump had just been averted. Rule-making and rule-breaking are the weft and warp of everyday life and the tension between daily life as a round of routine and obligation, brightened by the occasional liberating escape from it, gives the characteristic texture of everyday life. A routine is somewhat different to a rule, because it is more social, and because it more often involves other people, generally people we know, and as our routines affect theirs, so do their routines affect us. Sometimes we 'save' a bit of shopping for when we happen to be near a particular shop, district or person, or as something to do with them. Shopping for or on behalf of others can be burdensome, especially when it means catering for 'fussy eaters', but it is also an everyday opportunity to show that you keep a loved one in mind, know their food likes and dislikes and, as Daniel Miller (1998) observes, perhaps buy them a 'treat'. Even if we are not shopping for other people, or using it to show that we care, shopping is rich in opportunities for the brief encounter which can lift the day, such as some of the long-term light-hearted relationships which we develop with some shopkeepers.

What's real? What isn't?

For many years the domain of the everyday world was perceived as lacking any structure, or boundary, any set of institutions, or form of regulation, uniquely its own, and was thus seen as impossible to theorize. Then the social constructionist approach of Peter Berger and Thomas Luckmann (1966) dented this view and began to change the way structure was thought about, while feminist scholarship on women's lives brought to light the 'missing institutions', and most obviously the 'home'. The social constructionist approach revealed how the social world was 'made real', or solid and reliable, by individuals proceeding on the assumption that it was, and by investing confidence in social institutions. Confidence, however, is a fragile subjective state, and the substance of social institutions lasts only so long as the confidence, however 'solidified' and 'objectified' those institutions had become while individuals believed in them. But once confidence falters so does the institution, as was dramatically shown by the 2008 financial meltdown when banks around the world stopped lending to each other and global economic growth shrank back to the level of just after the 1939–45 World War. Though first described as a 'crisis of the banks' it was soon redefined as a 'crisis

of confidence and consumption' and the rescue remedy proposed
was that we should all to step up our shopping. However, the tax
cuts intended to keep the tills ringing, and aimed at the poor who
were thought more likely to spend any extra money which came
their way than the rich, who would just save it, did not work as
the poor, too, held on to their purses.

Not all institutions or structures are like banks and rest on solidity, or the hope of solidity, and some are essentially flexible, with
the market being, perhaps, the paramount example. Architects
build flexibility into buildings to that they can withstand shocks
and with Bruno Latour's (2005) call for sociologists to 'rethink the
social', to 'flatten' their view of society, 'stay close to the ground',
and trace the connections and associations which are made as individuals scurry around, the idea of the solid structure as the only
model has begun to wane in sociology too. Latour's emphasis on
structure as a trail seems almost made for shopping as something
which starts in the head as an idea or a plan, a routine, a need, a
want or a list, and does not end at the till, for the purchases have
to be taken home, shown, discussed and put away, or hurriedly
and secretly hidden, or even eaten before arrival. If shopping is an
endless trail, it is a self generating one, as it is very common to find
that, on returning home from a major shopping expedition, something has been forgotten, so another list must start. A basic tool
for dealing with everyday life, a shopping list, is a structure at the
back of the mind for many of us much of the day, and can lead to
the condition which one woman described as 'feeling a list coming
on', particularly in the middle of the night (Shaw, 1998).

The greater convenience which the longer trading hours of
today have afforded most of us has made shopping even more
central to everyday life, not simply because we do more of it,
but because as shopping has become more flexible it has become
embedded by being more 'combinable'. Shopping is the task most
often included in 'multi-tasking', and is, perhaps, 'doubled up'
most often with childcare, but with a laptop on the kitchen table,
shopping is increasingly also done online between mouthfuls. Just
before Christmas 2009 research by the money-saving website
VoucherCodes reported that seventy per cent of employees spent
time secretly shopping for Christmas gifts instead of working.

Flexible, interstitial and opportunistic, shopping constantly moves in and out of focus, and just as we pop in and out of shops, so shopping pops in and out of our heads as we remember to get more light bulbs, or presents for the children to take to a birthday party. Now more a spur-of-the-moment activity than a planned one, shopping is 'squeezed in' on the way to work, or way home, between dropping the kids off for swimming and fetching them again, or simply in the lunch hour. Sometimes life is still 'fitted around' shopping, as on a Saturday morning or Thursday evening, but shopping is more 'fitted in' than 'fitted around' and this changes its meaning. When trading hours were quite restricted, and it is worth remembering that only a generation ago shops closed for a half day mid week and all day Sunday, this increased a sense of the social order as 'out there', fixed and imposed.

Heroes and villains

Nowadays, though individuals are just as overworked and harassed, despite greater flexibility in working times and trading hours, the individual may feel a greater sense of choice and control in their life from something as simple as the freedom to change your mind about when to shop. The importance of time to everyday life is well recognized and Rita Felski (2002), among others (Rybczynski, 1991; Zerubavel, 1989), stresses that everyday life is effectively based on it. Shopping gave a temporal pattern and meaning to everyday life when opening hours were shorter, and it continues to now that they are longer. However the picture has also become more complex. Shopping is not as 'in your face' as it was in the era when billboards blighted city streets, though those billboards have been electronically re-established in our sitting rooms. Though, barring cyberspace, fully 24/7 shopping is still not universal, the use of shopping as a cultural currency has spread, been promoted and fetishized, not least by government in order to establish legitimacy for its privatization programmes, as if, for example, a lifetime of buying white goods and food were sufficient training when it came time for shoppers to find and fund a home for their elderly and ailing relatives, or, for that matter, to decide which water, gas or electricity supplier to go with. Our experience of shopping may actually not be that 'transferable' when it comes to buying a house or life insurance, but it serves us well as a popular currency. Read the headline 'Labour's plan for John Lewis public services', which will not make any sense to anyone who is not familiar with Britain, but for one who is, they will know that John Lewis is a chain of department stores which is distinctive in having an organizational structure in which staff are also shareholders and share in the profits.

We use our knowledge of shops to understand the world, to place people, and to invigorate our speech, so if we describe someone as 'shopping around' this is understood to mean 'not very serious', or if we talk of a 'one stop shop', this will be understood as bringing services together. Metaphor, George Lakoff and Robin Johnson (1980) explain, is what 'we live by' and by mapping one area of experience onto another we make new meaning. Though we may talk less today about being 'shortchanged', or 'left on the shelf', of something being done 'under the counter' or of 'shopping' someone, perhaps at the 'cop shop', new meaning is made when we talk of being 'shopped out' or off the 'top shelf'. Most metaphors linked to shopping are negative, though where traditionally the shopkeeper was the villain, as regulation on retail has tightened, people no longer need feel that they must be on their guard for sharp practice. One result of shopkeepers cleaning up their act is that the focus in shopping wordplay has turned to the shopper, increasingly pathologized and patronized as a 'shopaholic' or 'retail junkie' ever on the trail of 'retail therapy'. Indeed, it is the retailized society as a whole which is pathologized, with the idea that we live to shop. Which in the rich nations, we do. But this is because to live we have to shop, as most of us are citydwellers.

From Walden to Wal-Mart

With over half of the world's population now living in cities, self sufficiency, or a return to the 'stone-age economics' of barter is

not an option, and built-in obsolescence and technical advance
have largely removed the possibility of repairing more goods.
Judith Levine (2006) tried 'not shopping' for a year and, holed up
in Vermont well away from the temptations of New York, wrote
a book about her experiment. At the end of that year Levine cherished the more spacious feel which her Vermont lifestyle gave her,
and claimed to feel more secure; but even in Vermont she went
on thinking about shopping and though she did not actually shop
herself, her friends did so on her behalf. The moral issues which
had seemed so clear at the start of the year were much less so by
the end, and when Levine published her book she was roundly
censured for political insensitivity on the grounds that 'not shopping' was not a choice open to the majority. Still, Levine's tale is
important for helping to puncture the lazy assumption that the
spread of shopping is pandering to 'shopaholicism'. It is not 'shopping addicts' who patronize the petrol station or supermarket at
two in the morning but, as Barbara Ehrenreich (2001) points out,
cleaners, drivers and waiters picking up essentials before grabbing
a few hours' sleep. We learn from mistakes and Levine's mistake
was to think that one part could be excised from the whole of
which it was a part. While an interesting personal experiment,
it could not be scaled up, and retail, with the whole economy,
would go to the wall if we all stopped shopping, or even if just
those men who claim never to shop lived up to their word. There
is much to criticize about the economic system, capitalism, of
which most shopping is a part, but to scapegoat shopping, make it
the patsy of that system, is not enlightening.

Almost all of us who live in one of the richer nations buy and
own far more than we need, not just to live, but to live comfortably, and many of us are uncomfortable about this. Not because
having anything above the barest necessities is inherently immoral,
but because the uneven distribution of the world's resources is
unfair, and we know it. The sweated labour, much of it children's,
making cheap clothes in one country, which are bought and
thrown away after two wearings in another, before being packed
off as aid or charity to a third country where, on market stalls,
they undermine the livelihoods of local tailors, are clearly tragic
(Klein, 2000). However, so long as most of the goods sold in the

malls are largely made on the other side of the world, there is no escaping the fact that when shoppers rein in their shopping the consequences are felt not only in their homes but also in, say, the Vietnamese embroidery villages. Early in 2009, a friend visiting from Bangladesh asked how the recession was impacting in Britain, and was relieved when told that because the garment-making industries in her part of the world were focused at the cheaper end of the market, orders had not, so far, been cancelled. The rich countries do not wholly escape damage either. The relentless pressure to borrow more money, the hectoring 'last chance' sales and the shoals of junk mail, have made debt a painful way of life for many people, while the furtive targeting of children by corporations keen to capitalize on junior 'pester power' is immoral (Seiter,1996; Schor, 2004; Barber, 2007).

However the critique spun around shopping is often both confused and confusing as shoppers, shops, and the goods they sell, all come under attack at different times, with supermarkets especially criticized for their labour relations, treatment of suppliers, and effects on local communities and independent shops. Supermarkets have also been heavily criticized for many of their marketing strategies, such as the 'Bogof', the 'Buy one, get one free' offer which promotes both obesity and food waste, for hoarding land in hand for future sites, and for generally damaging the environment with plastics, pollution and over use of land-fill all the way down the supply chain (Gabriel and Lang, 1995; Simms, 2007; Blythman 2004). However, though supermarkets are the heavyweights, and have a huge share of the market, they are not the whole of shopping, and we probably use the corner shops as often, though do not spend as much time or money in them. We develop relationships with shops, often personalizing them, by referring possessively to 'my' butcher or 'our' supermarket, as well as relationships with people in them. Such relationships may be fleeting, but getting a tip from another customer in the supermarket about adding a pinch of ginger to meatballs or, as one friend does, practising her Hindi when she buys her daily newspaper, while not deep, can lift the spirit, and the day.

Negotiating a relationship: vegetables for two

I started this introduction with Charles Tilly's enquiry into the
sorts of answers which we give to the question 'Why', and his
claim that whatever reason we may give, what we are also in fact
doing is negotiating a relationship. This has led me to think about
what relationships I might be negotiating in writing this book,
and three possibilities spring to mind. First, of course, there is a
relationship with the reader, a student or colleague, but also with
experienced shoppers who will test every claim I make in this
book against their own experience; which I hope they will, but
also hope that they will come to see shopping in a different light,
and be interested in how other people experience, and do, it.
Then, there is the imaginary relationship with the critics who use
the word 'shopping' when they mean 'consumerism', and write
off shopping as if it were all about hopping on planes to New York
to buy clothes. Finally, there is a relationship with myself or, as
one wise friend, suggested, my mother.

At first, I was taken aback at this suggestion, though, like most
daughters, I did a lot of shopping with my mother and, in due
course, did a fair bit with my daughter, though she will, at the
same age, have done more with her friends. Shopping is done as a
way of negotiating relationships and it strikes me that today we do
more shopping with the generations on each side of us than we do
paid work with them, which is important for the reproduction of
culture. However, the key point about shopping and my relationship with my mother is that she was a tailor, and with her I spent
many hours in the London's West End, sometimes window shopping, of an evening, with our noses pressed to the windows, not
because we felt poor and excluded, but to discuss the finer detail
of the garments in them, and sometimes in the stores, usually the
fabric department. This has left me with a sense that an hour or
two spent looking around the shops can be as informative, enriching and relaxing, and even indistinguishable from an hour or two
spent going around some art galleries.

The personal world is, of course, also political, and feminism has
helped form my views about shopping, as it has for many of my

generation. However, much was done by second-wave feminists to expose what women's lives were really about; in particular, by drawing attention to the drudgery of housework, which includes shopping. But because of the all-powerful stereotype of shopping as women buying clothes and shoes for themselves, and the complicated relationship which second-wave feminists had with issues of appearance, they gave shopping a wide berth, leaving it to 'post-feminism' to reclaim shopping as a rightful pleasure. Hedonism is part of shopping and Colin Campbell (1987) cogently argued that it was every bit as important as any technological innovation in the first consumer revolution. However, due largely to the Puritan legacy, the West is very conflicted about pleasure, which is perhaps why Jonathan Gershuny (2000), who made the discovery about the scale of the time spent shopping, also found, when comparing diaries with questionnaires, that we systematically underestimate that time by at least half as much again. People who were asked about how much time it took them to shop just for food, estimated five to fifteen minutes, though they actually averaged sixty-three minutes, and those who estimated thirty to sixty minutes, averaged sixty-six minutes. Self respect might require us to shave our estimates for an activity widely thought of as a waste of time, and it might be thought that we always underestimate the time we take; but, of all the daily tasks measured, shopping stood out for this discrepancy. Yet, whether we love or hate it, think of ourselves as good or bad at it, we all take much the same amount of time shopping, which is why it is a mainstay of everyday life and our culture.

To get away from the negative and stereotypic view of shopping as 'rubbish', irresponsible and self indulgent, we have to take a longer view. Chapter 2, though not a history of shopping, attempts this by focusing on the history of the household and its evolution as a moral entity. The structural conditions which destroyed the household as a productive unit also transformed the meanings of production and consumption, and brought about a profound misunderstanding about their relationship too. If, at the collective level, culture, as in myth and history, is the repository of experience, at the personal level this is done by memory. We are lost without our memory, as we neither know who we are or where we are. Memories of shops and shopping are strikingly common as memories of childhood. Making then memorable are their associations with parents and the narrative shape of a shopping expedition which eases the telling of it. Telling anything shares an experience and something shared is usually something understood. Chapter 3 on shopping memories explores the how and why shopping is remembered, and how shopping memories help hold 'hold us together'. Shopping changes as we move through the life course, in relation to what we buy, when and where and, at critical points, shopping marks both personal and age-related milestones. Shops serve, informally, as schools, and drawing on the concept of 'situated action' Chapter 4 explores how new skills are practised or consolidated in shops, new boundaries tested, perhaps with a spot of adolescent shoplifting, and new identities are rehearsed or performed. A new wife or partner feels affirmed in her new identity by buying vegetables for two, a mundane event, but a shopping milestone and one which gives personal meaning and allows the woman to take her place in the culture.

If shops and shopping play a role in socialization they also play a role in reproducing culture. The key point about the 'situated action' approach is that the setting is as important as the person in it and Chapter 5 takes this further by exploring the part played by shops in facilitating the performance of gender, which they do because they are among the most gendered institutions encountered in the course of everyday life: by noting the gender of the shop we re-affirm our own. It is sometimes taxing for those not brought up speaking a language which is gendered to realize just how far the category of gender can extend beyond the human individual to shops and goods, and the scope for 'doing' gender which shopping as an activity offers. To be social beings we need to 'fit in', 'know our place' and have an idea of how other people work: stereotypes are the 'rough guides' which we use for this purpose sometimes by 'playing up' to those stereotypes, and sometimes by disavowing them. However, stereotypes or rough guides are also what we use to 'do' class, whether that is by putting on a 'posh voice' when we go shopping, or by feeling superior in the supermarket when we see what other people have in their shopping baskets. The shops which help hold us together are also where different classes are most likely to rub shoulders, and thus where class is done by looking and by being looked at by other people.

In writing this book I have, of course, drawn on my own experiences of shopping. However, I have also had the opportunity to draw on the observations and experiences of shopping as written about by the contributors to the Mass Observation Archive, and talked about from the people my colleague Janice Winship and I interviewed when we were researching what, at the time, we called the 'cultural success' of the British chain store, Marks and Spencer. In the midst of this project, the store suffered a major change of fortune, a hiatus, or period of troubles, from which a full recovery has yet to come and, in due course, this changed the focus of our project. As originally envisaged that project could not be completed, but it has, nevertheless, significantly shaped my thinking about shopping and explains why more references to that store than might be expected appear in this book.

The Mass Observation Archive is a British research organization which collects and archives first-hand accounts of everyday life and reactions to events of the day from a panel of volunteer writers. In the pantheon of research methodologies it is one of the 'peculiarities' of the English, and for accounts of how it operates, and how it has evolved, see Tom Jeffery (1999) and Dorothy Sheridan (1993; 1996). The strength of the material is the rich, discursive personal writing which is made possible by the relationship the writers have with the Archive, and is much drawn upon by social historians, sociologists, anthropologists and journalists.

I have also drawn on, and quoted, a number of writers of fiction and memoir whose descriptions of shops and shopping I have found particularly insightful. With this emphasis on the personal, the book is clearly not a meta-analysis of research on shopping, and is also distinctly British focused. Still, this does not materially affect the argument. If shopping can help us to hang on to ourselves, by serving as a container of memory, or shops serve as classrooms and a measure of personal history, they will do so not only in the British Isles. Similarly, if shopping helps us grow up and grow old, this will happen wherever we live. There may be more of a British bias in the discussion of class, because, arguably, there is more need in Britain for symbols to 'mediate' class divisions, because of their depth in British life, but class divisions are not absent from other nations, and certainly not in the United States. Taking the argument beyond the shores of Britain to the richer parts of Europe or the United States, shows how the long spell of economic growth in the second half of the twentieth century has led countries with a similar level of development to converge around a common lifestyle, and for that lifestyle to be based on retailization. Thus, except for the faces of people in the streets, shopping in Seoul today is, and looks, pretty much like shopping in Zurich and Chatanooga.

2
From Thrift to Spendthrift: How Buying Turned into Spending

'Anyone who tells you money can't buy happiness just doesn't know where to shop.'

Greetings card

'Don't Take the Squander Bug When You Go Shopping.'
Second World War Poster

'I shop and I shop!' Wailed Dot! 'And I still have nothing to wear!'
'Ethical' greetings card

'How can I avoid feeling guilty when I buy something?' says a married woman, knowing that her husband views her enjoyment of shops and shopping as moral weakness, while he benefits from her housekeeping skills and willingness to buy his clothes for him. There is no simple answer to this question, or to that asked by another woman, 'Is shopping for pleasure shopping?' The financial crisis of 2008 may, briefly, have helped recast the shopper as the 'consumer citizen' who keeps shopping in the national interest, but not so thoroughly that journalists have stopped writing about shopping as responsible for almost every social ill from political apathy through falling birth rates to rising rates of depression. With just one word, 'Prada', the media can make millions of women who have never seen, bought or could possibly afford, 'Prada' feel guilty/anxious/defensive about an activity which, like it or not, they are obliged to undertake. The reasons many women feel guilty about shopping, or spending on themselves, felt by many of them to be the same thing, are, of course, complex. These complexities are part of the relationships which the women and girls negotiate with themselves, their partners, their parents and their pasts. It is, however, the ancient past as well as the middle and more recent pasts which are critical for understanding how shopping, which was once a respected activity, and part of housekeeping, 'fell from grace' and came to carry in phrases such as 'shopping around' or 'reduced to shopping', the meaning of being either non-committal or thoroughly debased.

It is not difficult to demonstrate the low regard in which shopping is held today, but it was not ever thus, and it is because shopping was once associated with thrift, virtue and prudence, not profligacy, that this value reversal needs to be explored, for it interferes with an understanding of shopping as the social practice central to every day. Though in one chapter it is only possible to give some snapshots of the past, all epochs carry traces of earlier ones and, though millennia divide us from Homer and Aristotle, it is to their ideas that this discussion turns first, since much Western philosophy, especially moral philosophy, remains grounded in the ideas of the ancient world, and continues to exert an influence. We should, however, also look at patriarchy, and the 'cultural contradictions' surrounding pleasure and pain, work and play, which resulted from the impact which Calvinism had on the economic history of the West. This moves us, too, to the deepening of sexual divisions which followed as 'productive' labour moved away from the household in the wake of industrialization.

Each nation is unique, and all cultures have consequences, but there are commonalities in the impact which industrialization and, later still, de-industrialization, has had on societies around the globe. Crucially, as the smaller scale of household-based production gave way to the larger scale of factories and assembly plants, old livelihoods were destroyed. Some newer ones were created, but in every case a much broader social change ensued (see E. P.

Thompson, 1963). Just as what happened to the household is only part of the story, what happened to the household in Britain is also only part of a larger story; but I have focused on the household, because what happened to it, and to household production, was taken by moral philosopher Alistair MacIntyre (1981) as an exemplar for the concept of 'practice', the demise of which, in his view had been a turning point in Western history and a disaster for public morality. What happened to shopping or, rather, to the buying and exchange of goods, which turned into the much less honourable activity of 'shopping', was that the mix of tasks, relationships and behaviours which had comprised 'household production' disintegrated. Paid and unpaid labour became more sharply differentiated and, in due course, differently valued. This is almost a perfect example of MacIntyre's argument about 'practice', which he defined as a 'coherent and complex form of socially established cooperative human activity'. I am neither agreeing nor arguing with MacIntyre about whether the modern world has lost its moral compass, but some of the backstory to shopping's 'fall from grace' matches MacIntyre's argument about the loss of practice, so I use it to explain the poor public image, but not the practice of shopping, which offers those who do it plenty of opportunities to act in virtuous ways. But, for the sake of chronology, we need to step further back to the ancient worlds of Homer and Aristotle.

Prudence, patriarchy and practice make perfect

In Homer's time the household was the key social institution from which everything else, name, reputation, identity, honour and morality, flowed. Whether one was born or sold into a household, maintaining its honour and that of the kinsman at its head was a cause for which household members had to be prepared to die. In return, the household and the duty to seek its protection afforded household members the chance to show virtue through the proper discharge of their social roles, whether on the battlefield, as it was for men, or in the house, as it was for women. As then understood, there were four virtues: courage, prudence, temperance and justice, any one of which, if not displayed, would instantly turn into a vice. Courage, the supreme virtue, if not shown on the battlefield turned into cowardice, the worst vice; prudence, if not exercised, became profligacy. Later, as the concept of the polis took over from the household as the key social and political institution, Aristotle linked virtue to the quality of judgement exercised by the individual, and the effort put into living a 'good life', into thinking about others and about consequences, and thinking before acting, so that individuals did not just throw themselves bravely into battle.

Neither Homer nor Aristotle saw women as moral subjects though, through their misbehaviour, women might destroy a household just as, through their fidelity, they might save one. In both eras, virtue and vice were central parts of daily life and, as societies became more settled and wars waned, the skill, vigilance and calculation needed to survive the battlefield was transferred to the domestic setting where, as historian James Davidson (1998) details, a constant and minute monitoring 'through a series of ubiquitous practices' was required. Women as well as men were charged with knowing exactly how 'each cup should contain more water than wine, each mouthful more bread than meat'. Need and desire had to be brought into balance, something which continues to this day in a very practical way, for example, when calculating whether 'three for the price of two' is a bargain or a trap, and whether 'spending to save' is thrift or folly?

Traces of prudence and patriarchy, both central to the household in the ancient world, survive, though the household of course has changed. A much smaller enterprise than it used to be even two or three generations ago, the household today rarely comprises more than two generations, often only one and, increasingly, just one person. Household members today tend to be either kin or non-kin, rather than some of each, a major change from when more people, kin and non-kin, had to live together to survive, as both poverty and mortality drove the orphaned and the widowed to join other households as servants, companions, lodgers or apprentices. Today, as demographers define it, the household is a 'group of people who live together and pool resources to keep themselves warm, watered and fed'. While still seen as a unit of consumption, the household is no longer a unit of production, though home working has not quite disappeared; some people still earn their living by sewing, stuffing envelopes, running a small business, minding other people's children, walking their dogs, perhaps running a cannabis farm or a corner store. However, larger-scale home-based production for the market is non-existent in the West today, and with fewer home-made clothes and home-cooked meals there is less production for home consumption too. No longer seen as a place of work, home for more people is a place of escape from work. 'Home' is not the same as 'household', it does not command respect, allegiance or homage, and it does not outlive its members. It is not a cornerstone of name, reputation or lineage, with the possible exceptions of the House of Windsor, other royal families and the land-owning aristocracy. We may respect, as equals, those with whom we live, but we do not 'belong' to a household. When we did, the way we lived was different. With more people of different ages and statuses, social relationships within households were complex, as was the range of tasks done both within the dwelling and beyond. There was a mix of production for the market and for home and, with a high turnover of people, much readjustment around who slept where, when or with whom and, overall, much co-operation and interdependence. This was the household which represented 'practice' for MacIntyre until the industrial revolution swept it and its inhabitants away.

How buying turned into 'shopping': a new hysteria?

When discussing the effects on Western countries of the move from pre-industrial to industrial society it is useful to take Britain as an example, since it was the first nation to industrialize, while bearing in mind that nations which industrialized later did so at a faster pace, and could often skip stages. The crucial point is that as industrialization proceeded the new technologies and increase in specialization and scale drove production away from the home for both rich and poor. Cottage industry gave way to the factory,

large landed estates became uneconomic as their households
shrank, and housekeeping, the practice holding them together,
shrivelled with them. This did not happen overnight and in the
early stages of industrialization a good deal of paid work, weaving
especially, was done from home. In some of the early Lancashire
cotton mills whole families continued to work together, but
within the mills instead of at home (Smelser, 1959). Members
of a household continued to be supported by a mix of activities,
some bringing in money, some services by barter or exchange,
through board and lodging, and, say, childcare. The household
was still 'productive', and making for home consumption continued well after producing things at home for sale had ceased.
However, families found it much harder to combine childcare
with work and wives' contributions, economic and otherwise,
began to slide, at least in terms of how they were valued. The dis-
tinction between production and consumption sharpened and led
to categories of 'producer' and 'consumer' becoming both more
gendered and more unequally valued. Though there had been
nothing like gender equality in the pre-industrial period, each sex
had an absolute need of the other and would, if bereaved, usually
re-marry very quickly.

The tasks which made up housekeeping, however, were integrated with all the other activities which went on in and around
the house, and wives usually worked in fields, kitchen gardens
and workshops alongside their husbands. When a man came to
choose a wife he would consider whether she was, or would make,
a good housekeeper, just as much he would consider her likely
fertility. This mutual need produced a degree of mutual respect
and women were trusted to make economic decisions as well as
contributions. Spending and earning overlapped, and as economist
Tibor Scitovsky (1986) put it, they were 'traditionally divided
between husband and wife' because 'in the old days earning money
used to require strength and its spending shrewdness'. It was an
interdependence which produced a strongly co-operative social
form, exactly as MacIntyre describes, and as such was the basis of a
broader social and moral coherence. Once women were no longer
obviously contributing to the work which brought money into the
household, they were on the way to being seen more as undermin-

ing it, allegedly because of their propensity to spend unwisely. This is a major shift from an earlier era when women were respected for their skills, which included financial competence.

In most pre-industrial societies housekeeping, the practical administration of domestic affairs, was highly skilled, wholly estimable, and wholly necessary, in all households, rich and poor. There was no shame in the work of housekeeping, and many, even elite, wives were very proud of their housekeeping skills. Like the form of address 'Goodwife', being a 'good housekeeper' was a mark of respect and proficiency. Even today, the journal *Good Housekeeping*, with its 'seal of approval' based on testing products for the prudent housewife, carries some sense of this as a virtuous activity. In richer homes, a wife might not cook herself, but she would still know how food should be prepared; for example, that to fatten 'chickings' they must be fed milk and sugar and 'sewed up behind', and she would write it all down, which is why cookery books and household accounts are such a rich resource for historians. Writing of a gentleman's household in England of the eighteenth century, Amanda Vickery (1998) observes, that the household functioned like most commercial enterprises of the time and demanded planning, the management of staff, the keeping track of goods, accounts and bills, and knowing which tradesmen could be trusted. Purchasing, which was part of housekeeping, did not carry the same meaning as shopping does today, because for many centuries it did not involve going to shops, as very few shops existed outside of towns, and because surfaced roads allowing travel to them also barely existed. Purchasing was either from pedlars and hawkers who came to the house, or was a major, perhaps annual, expedition undertaken by men, who went to town and purchased the goods which their wives had told them were needed. Home was safer, and virtue, for women, meant them staying there.

Prudence, the virtue most obviously expressed through housekeeping, is part of shopping too, and is done by showing that you avoid risk. The dangers involved in going shopping were, until quite recently, very real: a messy, time-consuming activity, shopping meant venturing into the open air, or barely covered markets, which were often muddy, bloody, dangerous and licentious places, where you could be robbed, waylaid, tricked and sold adulterated goods, especially food, as well as soaked by the weather. You could also be seduced, as prostitutes found clients at markets just as much as other traders and, if you were a woman alone at a fair or market, you might be mistaken for a whore. A risk that was mitigated for some women traders by the sumptuary laws regulating what they could wear according to social status and which could, as art historian Evelyn Welch (2005) observes of Renaissance Italy, serve as protective clothing; and similar sumptuary laws, enforced at the same time in England had similar effects and codes.

Prudence remains part of the skill of shopping, though it is expressed today less through knowing how to detect adulterated goods, shaved coins, false weights, short change and rotten vegetables, than knowing where to shop and find a bargain. The skill once needed to judge if cloth was straight or skewed, just as wood would be, and know by touch and smell when vegetables or fruit were ready to eat, or sufficiently unready to survive storage, is not much called upon today but knowing when and where new stock arrives, or where there is a good outlet store is just as important. Shopkeepers, too, had to be prudent and wise to the tricks which shoppers played, stealing or damaging goods and bargaining for a reduction, failing to return excess change, and both buyers and sellers needed to know how to bargain, a skill which survived until fixed prices became common; which, in the United States, Scitovsky records, was introduced by Gimbel's department store in New York in the late 1890s.

Pride was taken in prudent purchasing, and it still is for, as old skills fall into disuse, new ones, such as knowing how to handle time-bidding on eBay, replace them. However, both the household and housekeeping had their heydays long before industrialization took root and, as Vickery notes of Britain,

> By the Restoration, the spread of wealth which meant that the stern hand of economic necessity was withdrawn from elite housekeeping, so ladies could devote themselves to spending money and the cultivation of ornamental qualities. Creative housekeeping decayed, the mistresses' skills atrophied and the ideal wife emerged in all her parasitic glory. Housekeeping became redefined as housework – that time-consuming drudgery best left to servants. Thus, between 1600

and 1850, it is often assumed, traditional housekeeping fell into a decline, thereby transforming prosperous housewives into inconsequential decorations and poorer respected workers into degraded skivvies.

(Vickery, 1998)

By the mid to late 1700s there was far less production and manufacture from raw materials, and household production was confined more to the 'final processing' of an ever-wider variety of goods purchased from retailers in a semi-finished state. In an aside aimed at fellow historians, Vickery further observes that the purse or 'pocket' – a separate item then not sewn into a garment – was far more emblematic of women's work than the more usual spinning wheel, and a mark, too, of the necessary financial skills needed for running a household. The 1800s are another chapter, and over the course of the nineteenth century women became increasingly compromised in relation to work, whether or not they were paid for it.

As women began to lose their foothold in the world of paid work, the sexual division of labour intensified, and the work women did, which had been understood as central to the whole enterprise, was no longer seen as such, so was devalued. It was then not long before women themselves began to be seen as superfluous, and an economic drain on the household. The link between buying and making, which had bound production and consumption morally, became attenuated. In practice all 'production' involves using up materials and labour, and most 'consumption' is also a production of something else. Cooking a meal uses material, labour and energy, but it produces something, a meal and a service, which is consumed, but this too produces something, good cheer, sociability, etc. But without a visible link, the moral axis revolved, so where 'making' was still 'good' and constructive, consuming or 'using up' was purely destructive and 'bad'. Though the volume of purchasing increased as a result of the industrial revolution and the consequent economic growth, 'buying' became associated more with 'non-working' women than with either men or the household. Without its tether in the workplace, buying became seen as shopping: more of a threat than a support to the household. The moral slide which ends with shopping standing for irresponsibility, wastefulness, hedonism, selfishness, materialism and an all-round meaninglessness had begun, and the ethical basis of everyday life changed.

The married woman and her money

Quite apart from work which might or might not earn them money, the relationship which women have with money is often quite disordered, not mentally, but socially. The historical reality, in many nations, is that as wives, sisters or daughters, middle-class or working-class, women have often had little or no control over money in their own right, and any money which they may have administered has been on behalf of the household, or its head, their father, husband or brother. In industrialized nations where well-meaning social reformers viewed women and children working in mines and factories as physically and morally unsafe, and rather less well-meaning early trade unionists were fighting for men's economic interests under the banner of the 'family wage', women had been pushed out of the labour market (Humphries, 1977; Horrell and Humphries, 1995). Not all women, of course, are wives, and even those who are, do not always have husbands in work, so the evacuation of women from the world of paid work forced many into the poorhouse or on the street. The assumption that money and men go together, but not women and money, continued in Britain as late as the last quarter of the twentieth century: a husband's signature was still needed to countersign his wife's for as routine a transaction as hiring a television. A regular theme of comic marital conflict in the popular 1950s US television series 'Ozzie and Harriet' was Harriet's need to ask her husband for money in order to shop. In a different context I still smart when remembering the estate agent who, in 1969, refused even to show me a house on the grounds that, as a single woman, I would not get a mortgage, so showing me a house would be a waste of his time.

During the nineteenth century, middle-class women were

increasingly sidelined by the doctrines known as 'the angel in the house' and the 'separate spheres', which relegated women to home and unpaid labour, leaving men with work and the 'outside world'. Made dependent on their husbands, fathers or brothers, middle-class women in the nineteenth century also presented what was known as 'the problem of surplus women', which made the unmarried or widowed feel guilty about their own existence. Gentility and gentrification added to all this. Middle-class women were seen to be 'demeaned' if they had to work, as some did, usually as governesses, while for lower middle-class families, or those of the 'labour aristocracy', a 'non-working' wife was crucial, first to raise, and then maintain, status. Thus while one in four married women were listed in the 1851 British census as employed, only one in ten were so classified in the 1911 census. In all likelihood, plenty of wives were still working alongside husbands in family businesses, but they were listed only as housewives and their economic contributions to those businesses were erased from the record. In contemporary US economics text books, we are reminded that when a man marries his housekeeper, national income falls because she is no longer considered as employed.

The 'angel in the house' doctrine should have led to a golden age of 'housewifery', but it did not and confidence in women's skills, including housewifery skills, diminished. But it did create an opportunity which was rapidly seized by the entrepreneurial pair Sam and Isabella Beeton, who, with a series of publications, began educating women from the middle and aspiring middle classes, in the practical arts of both housekeeping and social mobility. The *Beetons' Book of Household Management*, published in 1861, and later re-titled, *Mrs Beeton's Book of Household Management*, was the publishing phenomenon of the century and caught a wave of social change. Of Mrs Beeton herself, her biographer, Katherine Hughes (2005: 427), states that her mission had been to elevate domestic duties so that they could become something of which women could be proud of doing well. A 'doing well' which consisted, not just of the 'simple satisfaction in sparkling windows, a light sponge cake, and healthy children, but a genuine sense of competence that came from doing the whole thing on a budget'. Budgeting became ever more central to housekeeping; and though the advice given in the *Mrs Beeton* books was primarily practical, recipes, menus, table layouts and how to treat staff, sample budgets were also provided along with specific advice on products and where to buy them. The tone used towards their readers suggests an ever-present anxiety about failure to raise standards, getting things wrong, over-spending, and the need for a vigilance every bit as total as demanded in classical Athens, though it was more social gradation than need and desire which had to be balanced. The anxiety which the Beetons were stoking, rather than solving, focused especially on budgeting, not so much as 'making ends meet' but as a means of social mobility. It focused, too, on married women, not all women.

Not that the position of the unmarried woman was enviable; the position of the married woman was especially risky, most obviously because of childbirth, but also financially. For example, in Britain, the Married Women's Property Acts of 1870 and 1882 are rightly regarded as milestones in women's emancipation, allowing wives to keep control of any money and property they brought to marriage, rather than lose it to husbands who often then lost it altogether. The Acts were actually a sign of how much ground women had lost by the time the Beetons made their bid to restore it, and of how later attempts by women to recoup it would be met with resistance from the men, and create yet more anxiety within marriage. Then, as now, there existed a stereotype of the woman as the 'spendthrift', an interesting term and one almost exclusively applied to women, though the reality was that women had little access to or control over money, and it was men's profligacy which was the greater problem. In the mid nineteenth century single women, even independent and progressive ones such as Frances Mary Buss, a pioneer of girls' education who had set up the North London Collegiate School to help girls be more independent, needed obliging men to 'front' their ventures and hold bank accounts on their behalf since banks would not countenance lending women money in their own right. The assumption that men were more responsible than women where money was concerned continued until quite late into the twentieth century. Both in Britain and the US up until the 1970s husbands were assumed to be the head of household for the purpose of census records, and expected to return tax forms on behalf of their wives. To this day men exert more control over 'joint' money than their wives or partners, many of whom have no idea how much money their male partners earn. Utility bills are more likely to be put in the man's name, whether or not he is earning, or is even the home owner, and larger item purchases, such as cars, are likely to be registered in the man's name even if all or most of the money to buy the car was provided by the woman. The world assumes that men have money, even when they do not, and that any money which they handle is theirs to spend; but there is no equivalent assumption that any money which a woman has is hers to spend. This is why women's spending comes in for more criticism, direct or indirect than does men's, in much the same way as working-class spending patterns attract more public criticism than middle-class spending patterns.

With servants to do much of their household shopping for them up until the First World War, and for many middle-class women for some time afterwards too, most middle-class women in Britain were more anxious about spending money, especially on themselves, than were men of the same class. The first sentence of Virginia Woolf's (1925) novel *Mrs Dalloway* which starts, 'Mrs Dalloway said she would buy the flowers herself', can be read as indicating a departure from usual practice, or, with an emphasis on the fifth word, a summoning of courage. Shopping threads through this novel and illustrates some of the secret, imaginative forays which shopping allows, at least sometimes and for some women, as well as the very considerable anxiety which attended it too. Woolf herself was able to get on with writing the novel because someone else sorted out dinner, but in Michael Cunningham's (2000) novel based on a period of Woolf's life, chosen to illustrate the onset of insanity, he presents an episode in which Woolf, realizing that her sister is coming to tea, suddenly decides to send her servant 'up to London' to buy ginger.

Anxiety over shopping or spending on themselves is wholly embedded in marriage, as control over money leads to control over persons; so long as control of money is ceded to husbands wives feel, and are, trapped. For the generation of women starting married life up until, and for many some time after the end of the

Second World War, that life started with the wife keeping a close record of all household expenditure in a little book which could, and usually would, be looked over by her husband, whereas there was no convention of the wife scrutinizing her husband's expenditures. Again, barely a generation ago it was still common among the British working-class, or 'blue-collar' families, for a husband, after deducting a sum for his personal spending, his 'beer and ciggy' money, to 'give' his wife a 'housekeeping allowance' from which she had to meet all household needs. This 'breadwinner' model, as sociologist Janet Pahl (1989) describes it, left the wife with responsibility for, but without control over, money. Moreover, as 'the housekeeping' tended not to rise in line with wages, or prices, managing got harder over time. Even if, by scrimping and scraping, a wife, 'saved' a little, since no part of the 'allowance' was 'ear-marked' for the wife as her personal spending money, a very strong ego was needed before she could spend it on herself without feeling guilty.

Nonetheless, housekeeping should still have counted as virtuous, because it required planning, thinking ahead, and about others, being careful, and caring, frugal, the making and mending of clothes, as well as of food. But it did not. By the late nineteenth century the tasks which the wife undertook were not part of an integrated set of practices, and what she did, she did on her own, out of sight and out of mind from other members of the household. Indeed, some pride and pressure went into a wife having the meal on the table ready for the man when he came through the door, and making sure that he would find the children clean . and in bed, with all sign of their play, or production of the meal, cleared away. For a working-class woman, being a 'good manager' and 'stretching the wage' meant making meals out of 'nothing', a daily miracle of the loaves and the fishes, of keeping up appearances, and not showing the strain or how it was all done, preferably without spending a penny. Though the product, the meal, might be appreciated, the work and costs, human and financial, which went into its making were not. So, as Kathryn Hughes points out, wives were treated hardly any better than servants whose work was also meant to be out of sight. Husbands who never, or only rarely, shopped for household things, did not know how far prices had risen; and not knowing, or not being interested in how something is produced, or how much the materials needed to make it cost, encourages the idea that the person who pays 'silly prices' is herself silly.

The transformation of shopping from the virtue of thrift into the vice of the 'spendthrift', is currently embodied in the figure of the WAG (wife or girlfriend of a highly paid footballer), who is always pictured as barely visible behind a pair of large sunglasses and more shopping bags than she can carry. A snobbish caricature driven by envy of young women having money to spend on themselves and a traditional snobbish scorn of the 'nouveau riche', the WAG is offered as an example of how not to behave. Men, young or old, having money to spend on themselves is not a problem for other people, unless it all goes on drink and the children go hungry, and rich men are more likely to be offered as a role model than someone not be admired. The double standard is an old story and while more money goes on Rolexes and Porsches than shoes and handbags, this expenditure is not sneered at in the same way, and buying the large car is not seen as shopping. However, as 'nouveau riche', men can suffer too as the snub of one Conservative cabinet minister by another, as a man 'who had to buy his own furniture' shows; a snub enjoyed and exposed by another 'colleague' who had himself inherited a castle, and with it all the furniture he needed (see Clark, 1993). Wealth corrupts the wealthy, but even more, as it has appeared to several commentators, those who are not born to it.

In Western morality the notion of sin is conflated with excess, pleasure, superfluity, wealth and its corruptions. The surge in economic growth produced by the rise of capitalism, according to Max Weber's (1930) account, was the product of the austere and apocalyptic form of Protestantism adopted in the mercantile societies of northern Europe which presented them with a contradiction and a dilemma. Central to their creed of Calvinism, was the belief that all people were sinful, but that some were predestined to be 'saved' and go to heaven providing they led 'good' lives; but, in this world, no one knew if they were among the chosen. A second belief, more important in practical terms, was that the enjoyment of worldly goods was sinful. The combination of the two beliefs meant that the soundest strategy was to work hard and avoid sin in this world. The hard work bore fruit, but as the God-fearing merchants were forbidden by their religion from enjoying it, something else had to be done with its proceeds, so the merchants saved, that saving led to banks, the banks led to investment, and investment allowed enterprises to scale up, and capitalism took off.

The flood of new, plentiful, and relatively cheap, commodities across a number of European countries as capitalism, industrialization and colonial adventurism took off, created a moral crisis, the legacy of which is part of the story of shopping's moral journey. As new wealth and new commodities spread across Europe and became available to the bourgeoisie as well as to the traditional elites of monarchs, aristocrats and church, it later also came within the reach of the more lowly born. These were deemed incapable of appreciating the goods, but now were also at risk of being corrupted by them. New products always carry new meanings, and make older social and moral boundaries harder to maintain. They create anxiety for those who have most to lose from social change, namely their own privileged status, which they defend by promoting the idea that only those born rich know how to manage wealth and enjoy new commodities, especially luxuries, and remain uncorrupted by them. Clearly, a self-serving form of class antagonism, it was mingled and masked with spiritual concern for groups, initially the middle and later the lower classes, both seen as morally weaker, and in need of being saved from themselves. It was better that they were not allowed more than the bare necessities, for any more would undermine work discipline and lead to decay.

The moral threat was sometimes seen to inhere in the new goods, the tea, the coffee and sugar, which were seen as morally dangerous substances because they were pleasurable, habit forming, and so would lead to vice. Sometimes it was the spread of the goods to categories of people, lower-class men, or women of any class, who, first, did not deserve them, and, second, were weak and unable to exercise self control. The threat of the new, initially seen as moral, became political too. As wealth spread in the later eighteenth century it began to change both society and politics. For example, in Britain the latter shifting from court to parliament, and then spilling over on to the street and it was in the coffee shops, where newspapers and journals were read and discussed, that new and more democratic ways of expressing relationships emerged, at least for men (Berry, 2008). Writing of Holland during its 'Golden Age' of materialism, historian Simon Schama (2004) describes how the 'embarrassment of riches' which threatened damnation was only held at bay by a 'furious domesticity' and obsession with cleanliness and scourging at home. Schama interprets this as an 'enactment of the competing and apparently irreconcilable imperatives of Calvinism and humanism', as the moral conflict occupying the good burghers was dealt with by the 'properly run family household', seen then as 'the saving grace of Dutch culture'.

However, it was not only in seventeenth-century Holland that an embarrassment of riches led to a furious scourging, as Barbara Ehrenreich's (1989) analysis of the 'Yuppy' 1980s generation in the United States illustrates. The discrepancy facing the 'Yuppies', between the values into which they had been socialized by their thrifty post-war parents, of working hard, and repairing goods rather than throwing them away and buying more, seemed irrelevant, given their sudden access to wealth; but it also created an almost intolerable moral conflict. The yuppies were under great pressure at work, and also to work, play hard, consume hard, and look good. There was no time to repair things, and why should they? But they felt uncomfortable, and feared that if they got lazy, they would fall into the slobbish incontinent underclass, so they atoned with hard driven work outs. This is an example of what Daniel Bell (1976) called the 'cultural contradiction', meaning a problem of riches untempered by spiritual restraint which Bell traces to the 'sundering' of Puritanism from capitalism. It was mass consumption, unaccompanied by faith, which led to mindless hedonism, and loss of self control which would eventually destroy both social stability and moral coherence. A scenario now more or less condensed into 'shopping'.

Daniel Horowitz (1985), who takes Bell's argument as his starting point, charts a rather different story about spending and morality and, focusing on the United States, explores the gradual coming to terms with the spread of affluence. So, while spending was still seen by some to threaten discipline, both internal or external, rising living standards and mass consumption were seen as representing the possibility of mass self realization and happiness, increasingly required by democracy. While some commentators, for example, Thomas Hine (2002), see America as having joyously embraced the 'buyosphere' and all that it offers for self expression, others, for example, Tibor Scitovsky (1986), see the Puritan influence as still strong and that, without an indigenous aristocracy to represent a 'born to it' confidence in possession and enjoyment of luxury, American society remained deeply conflicted around the moralities and contradictions attached to making and spending. This returns us to the question of why women might feel more guilty, and more scapegoated, for their spending, than do men.

Coming at this from another corner, and drawing on her earlier work with Lynne Mikel Brown (1992) on the 'loss of voice' in young adolescent girls following the 'trauma' of their initiation into femininity, psychologist Carol Gilligan (2002) argues that there is a profound 'developmental and structural push' towards dissociation in the economic history of the West. For the individual, 'dissociation' means a mental compartmentalizing which often follows trauma and prevents a person from seeing connection for the culture it more often means ideology. Gilligan's evidence for this 'push towards dissociation' is based on her reading of the myths from the ancient world which leads her to suggest that Western culture silences women's experience, particularly around love, and leaves them split 'between image and memory'. Western women, Gilligan argues, are culturally required to deny what they know about relationships, in order that they become more biddable; so, as young girls turn into women, they come to act on one sort of knowledge, but not on another. It is a dichotomy which is produced by the difficulty, for women, of holding together what they are 'supposed to know', and what they 'really know' and leads to a difference between the story that we, or they, tell about themselves and the experience of what actually happened. If Gilligan is right, and there is a structural push towards dissociation, this may also have fed into the 'not knowing' which is part of shopping's fall from grace, not just a 'disconnect' between production, but also a 'disconnect' between how people behave in practice and how they talk about shopping and behaviour in the abstract. The loss of productive labour from the household was certainly a trauma, and it may have produced the ideological dissociation of 'not knowing' about the relationship between production and consumption which has fed the generally negative discourse about shopping. But the clearest evidence of this dissociation, and denial of the relationships involved in shopping, is the account given by Daniel Miller (1998) of how the very same people who one minute were showing and telling him how shopping was a task which they did for those they loved, carefully and frugally, and the next minute were describing all shopping as selfish, hedonistic and materialistic. Another example of this dissociation is laid bare in the press, the broadsheet press especially, where on one page all readers are addressed as potential shoppers, and offered advice on how to spend their money with 'reader offers', as well as plugs for particular items, and on another page presented with opinion pieces which describe the damage to the environment or society, or use 'shopping' as a term of contempt. For example, writing about a key forthcoming by-election, one columnist railed about voters behaving like 'shoppers not citizens', of 'using the ballot box as their customer complaints department', and 'treating their MP like a door-to-door salesman'. All because on the doorstep, the journalist had met a former Labour voter who was no longer certain how she would vote the next time, which led the journalist to wonder if that voter's support was 'conditional on customer satisfaction and whether she was "voting or shopping"'.

The assault on shopping is relentless, though often it is not the immediate topic or target, but it is populist and makes for an eye-catching headline. So, in a piece on the perils of cheap aviation fuel, picked out in bold is 'Some 92 million Bangladeshis could be driven out of their homes so that we can still go shopping in New York' (see Monbiot, 2007: 27). In another piece on 'the death of intimacy' and changes in family life, the claim is made that 'stripped of meaning, life becomes shopping' and that 'we no longer have real experiences, only voyeuristic ones'. During the war on Iraq, one column was headlined, 'Military families live in dread, while the rest of America goes shopping' (Younge, 2007: 25). The barrage barely falters as claims are made that millions are in 'thrall to shopping' and 'unable to find any other source of happiness or fulfilment' (Lawson, 2006), and that 'failed consumers' are turning to crime, without any evidence given to support a link between crime and the 'turbo-consumerism' under attack. Often the imagery used in the warnings directed at the public and at politicians is biblically apocalyptic thus, in a piece mainly intended as a criticism of the British government for adding to crime legislation, rather than focusing on reducing inequality, reference is made to the 'black reef of consumption and consumption crazed debt', a combination of false poetics and snobbery that is typical. A report on Chongqing, the world's largest growing metropolis, was used to build a picture of a world losing its bearings:

> As people move off the land and into the sky they produce less and consume more. In theory, they become socialized and civilized. In practice, they spend more time shopping and eating junk food. A nearby shopping centre, home to Kentucky Fried Chicken, could almost belong to any city on earth: pedestrianized streets, boutiques and fast-food outlets, a giant screen blaring out pop jingle ads, a monorail train running overhead. There are even police girls on roller skates, the latest must-have security accessory.
>
> (Watts, 2006)

This type of reportage is both patronizing and misleading, but it illustrates how shopping is positioned as a symbol of meaninglessness. What is actually wrong with pedestrianized streets, a mono-rail, or a police woman using roller skates, is never stated. Shopping is not, as implied by that piece, the whole of life, and it can give meaning as much as it might take it away. The ills implied are not real, they are not argued, and though women are not explicitly blamed, they are, indirectly, seen as culpable. That shopping is not allowed to be seen in a good light may have something to do with politics and journalism, neither field noted for being particularly women-friendly and the shopping implied, as in 'flying to New York to go shopping', is the sort of shopping stereotypically associated with very rich young women shopping for clothes who, to some critics, might seem fair game. Gilligan's point was that dissociation helps to silence any expression of a pleasurable, loving and life enriching experience. The sort of reporting described above achieves this and perhaps, needing a soft target, the commentariat turns on shopping and intentionally or not makes half of their readers feel uneasy and scapegoated.

Practice revisited

There are many twists and turns in shopping's moral journey, of which the rise of 'ethical' shopping, and the limited rehabilitation afforded by the 2008 financial crisis which recast the shopper as 'citizen consumer', are two recent examples. Perhaps shopping could return to an earlier state of grace based on something closer to the integrated 'practice' which moral philosopher Alistair MacIntyre (1981) argued had all but disappeared from the modern world? Not, of course, to anything like the integrated practice of household production before the industrial revolution, but shopping is part of what makes modern life meaningful, and it provides some opportunities for virtuous behaviour. For MacIntyre it was practice, based on co-operative endeavour, which provided the internal 'goods', the trust, grace, well being, achievement, reputation, respect, satisfaction in a job well done, community coherence, joy in seeing plants and animals thrive and the harvest brought, which then held people together, not just the work. They were 'internal' to the practice, and when that went, so did they, and their loss meant that virtues tipped over into vices just as Aristotle envisaged.

Practice, as seen by MacIntyre, offered the individual a chance to live a 'good life' in an 'ethical' way, though he made clear that it was not enough for individuals to embody virtue in their daily activities for the broader moral integrity which could result, and that a range of 'supporting institutions' and skills also needed to be present in the population at large. While MacIntyre might not have seen shops, or shopping, as virtuous, some shops might qualify as 'supporting institutions'. Among these are the Co-op, perhaps most obviously, but also Christmas clubs, consumer affairs programmes and publications which in Britain would include *Which* magazine, and radio programmes such as 'You and

Yours' or 'Money Box Live', and internet 'switch' sites. US and Canadian examples of consumer cooperatives include Recreational Equipment Incorporated and the Mountain Equipment Co-op. As a daily practice, shopping obviously involves virtue, both as in thinking about others and as duty. The whole charity, or thrift shop sector should count as a 'practice', as it affords many of those who participate in it, donors, workers, volunteers and customers, the sort of 'internal goods' commended by MacIntyre: grace, satisfaction, a sense of a job well done. Supportive of good causes and recycling, the charity shop provides opportunities for voluntary and co-operative labour, draws customers and workers from across the class spectrum, and enables them all to feel part of a larger whole. It raises awareness of the particular charity, makes donors feel better and districts look better if the alternative is a boarded up shopfront. But to illustrate exactly how virtue in MacIntyre's terms might lead to the sort of virtue and internal good which he commends, I offer the case of the pensioner in my home town. Each week this old lady calculates how much she needs to live on, then with what remains, three or four pounds, she scours the 'charity shops' for the 'best buy'. When she finds it, she buys it, and then goes straight to another charity shop and donates it. In this way, she says, she 'gives twice over'. Of course, she could just drop the money in a collecting box, but does not; because she likes going around charity shops, and likes to support them in a practical way. She had worked in one herself when younger and knew that most of the staff, certainly all the volunteers, got much satisfaction from their work, and especially from seeing people find 'good things' at reasonable prices. It is also illustrates the point which Alvin Gouldner (1973) makes about the importance of 'something for nothing' as triggering, along with its companion 'norm of reciprocity', a benign cycle.

Though in general deeply pessimistic, MacIntyre (1981) saw some hope for the future of the modern world in narrative, in 'the told, intelligible account of our actions by and of ourselves' which he thought could revive a mutually sustaining cycle. Arguing that thinking of a human life as a narrative was thinking in a way which was 'alien to the dominant individualist and bureaucratic modes of modern culture' he outlines how the 'good' of a whole human life, conceived of as a unity, could transcend even the limited goods which come from practice. A very abstract argument, and one which cannot, in every detail, be mapped onto shopping but, as we will see in the next chapter shopping is pretty good at capturing memory and generating the stories which help us to make sense of our daily experience. The stories we tell of shopping, the finds, or failures to find, the bargains, the rude or the helpful assistant, as part of everyday conversation support everyday civility. We note which shops have closed, which new ones have arrived, we note changes to layout, some which we approve of, and others about which we complain. If, as a woman, we receive a compliment from another woman, about something which we are wearing, nine times out of ten we will reply with a story of how we came by it, how much it cost, and if the other woman seems interested to buy one too, we will give an assessment of her chances. For the item has a history, and the context requires that the history be told, for shopping, as well as the goods we buy, have a narrative form and encourage a narrative telling. The capacity of shopping to generate narrative is part of what enables it to give meaning, and it is through narrative, as Jerome Bruner (2002) has argued, that we create our selfhood. The self, Bruner argues, is 'a product of our telling, not some essence to be delved for in the recesses of subjectivity' and selfhood, and, Bruner, continues, we 'cannot proceed without the capacity to narrate', for it is the telling which 'gives coherence and continuity to the scramble of experience'. Both Bruner and MacIntyre stress the importance of narrative for creating meaning and for Bruner, especially, narrative and culture are one and the same. It is culture which gives us the template of narrative which allows us to tell stories about ourselves, and through that telling to make and remake ourselves. Not all our stories are about shopping, but shopping is something we can all talk about, as we do, even if to maintain that we 'never go shopping' or 'hate it'. For shopping is, as Sharon Zukin (2004) describes it, a 'talkative practice', and by being so helps to make everyday life a little bit more sociable, a little more co-operative and a little more committed.

3

A la Recherche des Shops Perdus

'One of my earliest memories is of shopping with my grandmother. As we reached the greengrocer's, she said, "We must buy a pomegranate, Auntie Elsie's coming for the weekend." I do not know about other fruit bowls in the 1960s, but I had never seen a pomegranate.'
First line of the obituary for Elsie by her niece Ann Gorecki, *Guardian* 'Other Lives' 7.10.2008

Ask someone over a certain age about their 'first memory of shopping?', and few will hesitate before launching into a vivid tale of living over a shop, buying sherbet lemons and liquorice laces, getting lost, lunching with mother in a department store, or the delight (if coming from a large family) of getting her to yourself for once. As memorable as the first day at a new school, shops are powerfully evocative places and 'going shopping' is a template for adventure. Unless we were brought up in a remote rural area, we will have had experience of shops and shopping long before we learned to walk, talk or go to school. We may not remember ourselves being cooed over by strangers, lifted out of a pram or pushchair, or more recently a 'buggy', too bulky to push into a shop, or stuffed into a trolley, even passed around, but most of us will have witnessed such occasions and can imagine how formative it might be. As shopping is the domestic task most often, if not always most easily, combined with childcare, shops are for many children the outside world, and are visited more often than, say, other people's homes. Even if not city kids we are likely to have memories of playing at shops, or of having 'toy shops', of 'treats' for being good in shops, and punishments for not, and for an older generation, running errands to shops for our parents, even as young as four years old. We may also remember other, now extinct, traditions such as butcher shops with sawdust on their floors, which could be played with and pushed into piles or patterns, or the canisters in old-style department stores which shot money and receipts across the ceilings on pulleys and wires, or through pneumatic tubes, or the machines for taking X-rays of feet, which were once an essential and thrilling part of buying shoes, though some children found them terrifying; and many shops assistants died of cancer through constant exposure to the radiation. Not all early shopping memories are benign and the trip to see 'Father Christmas', a promised reward for 'being good', was often not only disappointing, but also rather frightening and disturbing.

Memory is our personal investment in the past, but it also helps us to negotiate the present, for without memory we simply do not know who or where we are. Though memory is not a faithful reflection of the past, it bears some relation to it, and can help us keep a hold on our personal identity. Memory allows and encourages us to reflect upon and learn from experience, which is necessary if we are to plan for the future. However, memory needs help, it needs a prompt, and as psychologist Jerome Bruner (1960) noted, 'the most basic thing that can be said about human memory is that unless detail is placed into a structured pattern, it is rapidly forgotten'. The ease with which people can supply memories of shopping shows, at the very least, that shops and shopping are memorable and the question for this chapter, is what is it that makes shops and shopping memorable? The short answer is that, as an activity, shopping has a narrative shape and structured pattern and, moreover, because it is both familiar and familial it is very evocative. As fixed points in the landscape, shops can and do often serve as 'containers' of experience and as a well-trodden bridge to the past, shopping is something which most people can easily imagine themselves doing in earlier eras, more easily than, say, labouring as a stone breaker or chimney sweep. Much of the character of the past is bound up with shops: 'The Toggery' moth-balled in Wilcox, Arizona, survives as a museum/memento of the 'frontier era', while other shops, such as the old 'cork' shop in Brighton, England, was removed to the local museum. Drawing on autobiographical accounts and reminiscences of shops and shopping, this chapter shows how shopping is used to construct or restore a sense of personal identity.

Stardust and sawdust

The practical 'scaffolding' which shopping provides us with, by shaping our daily rhythms and routines, is repeated as memory or mnemic. The social historian Orvar Lofgren (1998) describes how, when collecting life histories, he developed the habit of asking his interviewees for memories of consumer items, a technique which, he says, he owes to a character in a Margaret Atwood story who declared that it was 'impossible for me to remember what I did, what happened to me, unless I can remember what I was wearing; and every time I discard a sweater or dress I am discarding a part of my life'. Resisting the urge to discard parts of oneself seems pretty healthy and, for all the modern emphasis on 'letting go', a sense of continuity, or history, is essential for identity, both per-sonal and collective. Lofgren refers to goods, and what they mean for individuals, not to where they might have been bought. But in much the same way shops, and memories of shops, are bound up with who we are and how we came to be who we are. Long-established shops store and preserve something of ourselves so that when they depart, some part of us does too. While I was working on this book, the Co-operative Society in Great Britain decided to close all its department stores and, since I lived close to one of them, which was 'run down' over two or three years, I have heard, and taken part in, much talk about the store, its closure, and what might happen next. People knew that it was terminal, and displayed the same sort of behaviour which they would with a friend or relative who was dying: trying, in turn, to be stoic, sympathetic, pragmatic, worried about what would happen to the store, the remaining staff, themselves, and the area. My builder talked about it in the present tense, resolutely telling me that he still buys 'his toys' there (meaning toys for his children), because it was where he was taken as a child to get 'his toys' and to see Father Christmas.

Of course, things change and, of course, we resist much of it deliberately, if it does not suit us, as the volume of complaints when supermarkets alter their layouts illustrates. However, change in or to shops is special because we feel it personally, which is part of the reason why we remember shops and shopping as well as we do. Though we might think of memory as factual recall, it is really a very highly edited and partial re-construction of the past, and one which serves the present more than the past. Few people can remember much before the age of two and the ability to tap memories related to early experience depends upon cognitive and language development. One friend describes her first memory, at around the age of two, as being in another house and of reading, or, rather of having a book read to her. Another has a very vivid recollection of staying in a public house, somewhere on the outskirts of London for a few days when he was about seven, but without his parents. In both cases the memories seem very sharp, but also de-contextualized. The woman was not able to make sense of her memory, other than knowing that it referred to the night her younger brother was born, and then added that for the first four years of her brother's life she totally ignored/denied his existence. For the man too, he knew that in some way his sojourn in that public house was linked to the seven-year gap between him and his next sibling.

'Screen' memories: lost and found shops

Though Freud (1901) thought that nothing was ever really forgotten, he also thought that what we forget, or repress, is as, if not more, important than what we remember; and writing specifically on memories of early childhood, Freud made displacement and dislocation the key to what he called the 'screen memory'. This memory, very mysterious and fragmentary, typically involves one very sharp, vivid often physical detail which does not quite make sense, and indeed, is innocuous, and that is its point. It is there to 'screen' or hide some deeply troubling event or experience, and all the intense feelings surrounding it which are too difficult, painful or humiliating to remember directly. Those feelings, however, are preserved with all their intensity by being displaced on to some other more innocent element of the original event, for example, perhaps, the public house, or 'being read to' and which, sometime later in life, we might decode. Not all anxiety, shame and embarrassment is displaced, whether in relation to shopping or something else, but shopping is often remembered for the agonies of the communal changing room, of asking for a larger size and being told that the shop does not carry them, of mix-ups over change, getting the wrong end of the queue, or, as one friend was brutally told, on entering a fairly up-market kitchen shop, but wet through from a sudden downpour, 'Madam, I don't think we have anything here for you.' Still, not all memories, even ones as vivid as these, are screen memories, but the very sharp 'telling' detail is important of many of them.

A retired midwife writing for Mass Observation describes her earliest shopping memory, as 'rationing', and what she called the 'points system attached to some goods, and the clothing coupons'. Rationing, which had been introduced in the First World War for basic foodstuffs, was extended during the Second World War to ensure that everyone had access to an adequate supply of food, clothes, furniture, medicine, not just those who could pay high prices, and the 'points' reflected need, so, for example, in Britain, children got more points for eggs than adults, while in the United States, during the same period, canned milk was reserved solely for children.

The points and the ration cards were a routine part of everyday shopping, as too, were the queues. However, more particularly, the midwife remembers her mother 'rubbing out the pencil crosses on their ration book' for the greengrocer 'so we could get extra'.

She explains that the greengrocer had been an albino, and had poor sight, and then writes, 'In retrospect I am not proud of my mother's actions, but things were hard then. There was a system of bartering rather than shopping. We exchanged eggs and rabbits for goat's milk, and everyone who was able had a vegetable garden.' The woman remembers the ration book and the pencil crossing out, but it is the hardship as much as the feeling of shame at her mother for taking advantage of the greengrocer which fixes the memory and in the next sentence she describes, 'When sweets were to be de-rationed they were only in the shops very briefly because everyone bought as many as possible, so again, there were no sweets to be had.' Rationing, of course, was not a uniquely British experience and existed throughout Europe. In the United States food rationing was introduced in 1942 and lasted until the end of the Second World War and children who lived during that period will remember the 'Sugar Card'. As a child, sweets are a particularly strong memory, and the day that they 'came off the ration', rather than the day on which 'the war' ended, are the 'iconic' memories.

The telling detail is the hook that pulls the memory from the deeper recesses and leads to a telling of the story, a telling which both fixes and shapes the experience. One of the reasons why life-history work is used therapeutically with older people is that encouraging recollection of the past helps a person whose memory is failing to hold on to themselves by holding on to the past events which had made them who they are. Telling a memory, like telling a dream, fixes it, at least for a while; however, the telling is also shaped by the way it is told which, in turn, is shaped, by the codes and conventions of telling, the catalogue of storylines, which are part of the culture of the teller. Early in his memoir *A Tale of Love and Darkness*, Amos Oz (2005) asks 'What does memory begin with?', then answers by telling the reader that, for him, Oz, it began with a shoe, 'a little brown fragrant new shoe, with a soft warm tongue'. 'It must have been one of a pair, but memory has only salvaged that one.' A shoe so entrancing that Oz put it on his face, felt drunk with the smell of it, and was photographed for being so cute. It was a shoe which had survived in the pleasure of a foot tentatively entering the inner walls of that first shoe, and is recalled to this day every time Oz pushes his foot into a shoe or boot. But Oz's second memory is far less benign. He had been sent to a child-minder who often 'dragged' him around to various clothes shops where she tried on garment after garment, dresses, skirts, negligees and a fox fur, but without ever buying any of them. On one of these expeditions Oz is bidden to sit still and wait obediently, but he catches sight of a girl and, fascinated, follows her past bales of cloth 'down a tunnel-like passage lined on either side with tall tree trunks festooned with dresses, branches of the women's world, a dark fragrant·maze of warm paths, a deep seductive silky, velvety labyrinth that ramified into ever more dress-lined paths. . .'. Oz gets lost in this 'forest' and, as an adult writer explicitly plays on the motif and imagery of the fairy tale, the valiant knight and the fair princess, the need for courage and to overcome the monster. However, Oz, the child, soon discovers, to his horror, that the girl he has followed into this labyrinth of the unfamiliar, is not a child, but a dwarf witch (an older midget) with incisors like a fox. Running for his life through this tunnel in the store, the young Oz finally finds a niche, the size of a kennel, in which he can hide. Eventually Oz is rescued by a 'kind old Arab man' and, after having somehow acquired a retractable tape measure, which he calls 'the good snail', Oz survives his ordeal in the mysterious and Freudian underworld of a female clothing store.

Stories of being lost in shops are very common, and one friend recounts of how, aged four, he had become separated from his mother in a shop; then, knowing that they had arrived by train, he somehow, alone, found his way through the vast streets back to the station, and even attempted to board a train, before what he called the 'station police' took charge. The tale of being lost in the shop is one of the archetypal narratives or story forms, with its journey into the unfamiliar, its sense of threat, escape, rescue, and then a reunion. Child psychoanalyst Anna Freud (1969) uses the example of a child getting lost in a department store to illustrate a broader thesis about the meanings of losing and being lost. We tend to lose things in shops, umbrellas, gloves, purses, and our reaction to such losses, often being cross with ourselves, is partly because losing things is a version of losing ourselves. Sometimes, of course, when we go shopping we set out to 'lose ourselves', as we might seek to 'lose ourselves in a book'. As enclosed spaces shops have the potential to change us by inducing a form of free association, which we indicate when we talk about 'mooching around' in shops, in other words, 'reverie' or daydreaming which might lead us to discover something about ourselves and our desires.

Walter Benjamin (1999) described the grand Parisian Arcades, around which he had been reluctantly dragged as a child, as 'dream worlds' and 'phantasmagoric'. He was also very critical of them for burrowing into the minds of the shoppers and builds a critique of consumerism on his analysis of their pernicious effects. Rosalind Williams (1982) takes up the baton and writing of the same Arcades as 'dreamworlds' argues that, overflowing with goods, experiences and exotic displays, they were *designed* to arouse a free-floating desire-induced irresponsibility, partly by encouraging the fantasy of a return to the womb, only in this case a 'womb of merchandise'. The point is the disorientation and while people enter shops, both with the intention to buy and to not buy, in both cases the very opposite often happens. Shops and shopping change us, and we prepare to be changed by them in various ways. People used to dress up to go to the shops, put on hats, gloves and accents and, though this is no longer a convention, people still act up in shops, often smiling or pouting at themselves in mirrors if trying on clothes.

Finding ourselves in shops

If we can lose ourselves in shops or by going shopping, we can also find ourselves, or part of ourselves in them too; and if shops can produce confusion and disintegration, they can also restore pride, confidence and self respect. Writing of her mother's last, difficult years suffering from Alzheimer's disease, Linda Grant (1998) describes how her mother Rose seemed, if only briefly, to become 'a proper person again' inside a shop. Her mother's identity, as it seemed to Grant, 'reformed itself around the undamaged, coherent centre, or the part of the brain which controls our urge to shop' when she was in a shop. Grant acknowledges that this is a fanciful idea and adds she had 'not been able to locate this area on any diagrams, but I know it must exist'. The unexpected 'recovery' could have happened anywhere because of a general capacity of social context to affect the inner world, and potentially any shop might serve as a 'container' of experience, memory, confidence and identity.

It was perhaps no accident that Rose began to feel a bit more her old self in Marks and Spencer because of the place which the store, a household name, occupied in British culture as well as in Rose's life. Its founders, like Rose, were Jewish, and the glory years of the store had coincided with hers so, both through what the store symbolized, and what it gave her practically, for example, a familiar layout, it could 'scaffold' her and temporarily help to restore her. It occupied a privileged space in her internal world and was where Rose's youthful, confident and competent self still had a foothold. Being a 'good shopper' had been a major source of pride for Rose and, as her daughter sadly notes, not only did her mother's memory seem to have been formed around the urge to shop, but 'her capacity to match navy was preserved long after she could not distinguish the difference between her daughter and her long-dead sisters'. Her skill at shopping was part of her cultural capital, hence a trip to the store was restorative or 'capacity building' because it allowed her to do the sorts of things she wanted to do, and be the sort of person she wanted to be. The familiarity of the store which helped with Rose's recovery also eased relations with her daughter, who could then play her 'part' too. In another passage Grant observes how, despite all the difficulties which went with caring for someone suffering from Alzheimer's, she found that she could still love her mother when they shopped together:

> we lose ourselves and the past and the future in a department store – nothing that belongs to time is of any significance except the rise or fall of the season's hemlines or its shades or the width of lapels or the colour of lipstick. So we shop together, outside time, mother and daughter united each in our purposeful quest to do what we have always done, and which to her goes on making sense: That would suit you, Mum.

Memories of shopping with Mother

For obvious reasons, many childhood memories of shopping are connected with parents, mothers especially, and with shame and embarrassment too. Even in adulthood, shopping with mothers can be excruciating, as one man recalled it was for him when, going to buy a bed which his mother had offered to pay for, meant that she came too and lay beside him on several beds to test them, a horrible Oedipal moment. Mothers may be embarrassing, but so is poverty and coming together as they did for Jenny Diski (2002) when taken by her mother to buy a pair of shoes before starting at a new school, not with money but a voucher supplied by Social Services, was excruciating. A dreadful experience for both of them, it was a matter of desperate shame for Diski's mother, as it returned her to a poverty which she had 'devoted her life to escaping. The idea of handing over – in public – vouchers from the state instead of crisp currency agonized her. Worse, the vouchers were rejected with the disdain she feared at all the shops to which she usually went, as 'Daniel Neal did not X-ray any old child's feet.' The only place which accepted the vouchers was 'a gloomy little cobbler's shop' which, as Diski remembers it, 'was hidden away under a near derelict railway arch in the fashion wasteland of King's Cross'.

Alert to the Dickensian association, Diski wonders if it was a false memory conjured up to match the dismal mood of the event, as the only shoes which were offered to her were the 'grimmest black lace-up school shoes' she had ever seen, for which 'sturdy' did not get close to describing their 'brute practicality . . . great clumping virtuous blocks of stiff leather with bulbous reinforced toecaps, designed . . . never to wear out'. Diski continues with the 'bubble of ancient hysteria' welling up and remembers how she felt that if she wore them they would stand for her entire character and 'for ever after my almond-toed peers would deem me a sad case to be avoided and sniggered at as I clunked my solitary way around the playground'. It was not just the 'social disaster of being unfashionable' which distressed Diski, but the fear of appearing to be the kind of person who wore such shoes might mean that she actually was that person, so she would thereafter despise herself as well as being despised by others. So Diski politely rejects the shoes but, taking a stand, tells the old man that she has seen through his attempt to off-load his unsaleable stock, a sally which he ignores, and repeats his question of whether she wants to try another size, and makes clear that with the vouchers there is no choice. By this time her mother is near to hysteria with embarrassment, and Diski refuses to try any more shoes, so they leave feeling that the world is about to end. There are hints of Cinderella as well as Dickens in this recollection, and Diski rages at being made to feel that being in need of the voucher she and her mother were assumed to have brought their fate on themselves by being careless or profligate, and so should be stigmatized, made ugly and denied choice as punishment. The dreadful shoes were eventually escaped from, but they remained a terrible memory and brought back the intense feelings of hatred, shame at needing charity, and the impossibility of self respect if you were poor. It was a continuation, in effect, of the principle of 'less eligibility' established by the 1834 Poor Law, meaning that life was to be made harder for the recipient of charity than that of even the poorest labourer.

Shame, shoes and class

The importance of decent clothing for self respect was understood as long ago as 1776 when Adam Smith wrote of how 'a linen shirt was necessary for a creditable day labourer not to be ashamed to appear in public'. Shoes are the equivalent today of the linen shirt, and social class is more accurately 'told' by footwear than by any other item of apparel, which is why shoes and handbags are items upon which many otherwise financially sensible folk will 'over-spend'. Diski's experience of the acute shame which accompanied this particular memory of shopping was probably further intensified because it was associated with shoes, which in many cultures, are especially potent symbols. Having to wear second-hand shoes is more shameful than wearing second-hand clothes, or patches on your elbows. Footwear traditionally marks the boundary between nature and culture by protecting a person from dirt and uncleanliness and is why, in caste systems, leather workers and tanners are among the lowest of the low, why pointing one's feet at another person's head is the ultimate insult, and why there was a furore when a journalist at a news conference in Iraq threw his shoe at President G. W. Bush, and aimed it at his head.

Folklore and fairy tales testify to the special place of footwear as fetishes. Cinderella's elevation came about through a slipper, there was the Old Lady Who Lived in a Shoe, Oz's first memory was of a shoe, and aside from any sexual connotation which shoes might carry, as objects they lend themselves to symbolization because they are small, and small objects condense meaning more effectively than larger ones, because they are easily manipulated.

Though I no longer have any of my children's baby clothes, I still have my daughter's first pair of shoes, and remember exactly where they were bought, on the Isle of Wight, and how she slept through the whole process of fitting and buying. Discussing why some artefacts or events, clothes, music, a book, a film, a demonstration or rock concert, come to be deeply invested with meaning for a whole generation, Christopher Bollas (1992) argues that it is because the items or events symbolize their moment of entering adulthood, so he calls them 'generational objects'. Shops can serve in this way. For many women of 'the 1960s' generation, if they had lived within reach of one of the Biba stores in or near London's Kensington High Street, the store might be such an 'object', just as much the knee-high mauve suede boots it sold, now fondly remembered as much for the feelings of freedom, energy and hopefulness which they represented as for the feel and look of the suede; and evidence that those boots do revive such feelings is perhaps reflected in the prices they now fetch on eBay. 'Store', of course, is another term for a shop, and by coincidence the shop reputed to have inspired Charles Dickens's novel *The Old Curiosity Shop* is sited in Store Street, London, and when I last passed it, had become a shoe shop. All symbolization is based on meaning becoming condensed, and part of what makes shoes and little shops memorable, and useful as symbols, is their small size.

Feeling small is part of the experience of childhood, and is also a part of the feeling of being 'put down' for being working class;

and some considerable internal struggle is often needed to maintain self respect when low social status is an objective reality, and as among the settings in which individuals are made to feel especially self conscious, this is often a feature of memories about shopping. For example, a retired teacher writing for Mass Observation began his account of remembering shopping with, 'My shopping memories go back nearly to a time . . . when Sainsbury's shops were rectangular with white counters behind which chiefly male assistants served goods. These were laid with porcelain tiles, rather like those to be found in better public lavatories. My family rarely used such establishments, partly because they seemed to cater for a higher social class than ours, but also because my father worked for a much smaller rival establishment which provided, at reduced costs, the bacon, eggs, sausages, butter and ham that we needed.'

It is an account which makes very clear the relationship between class and where you shop, and details which, for this man, stick out about the shop, the rectangularity of the counters, the men serving behind them and the hard shiny surfaced porcelain tiles, also represent hardness, masculinity and non-negotiability of the social order. Of course, the same details carry other meanings too, and the tiles, in particular, spelt 'modern' and 'hygienic' as well. Life was just as hard for a retired, now widowed, typesetter, and he was just as short of money much of the time, but born, perhaps, with a sunny disposition, he gives the lie to J. K. Galbraith's (1958) claim that the poor man always has 'a very precise view of his problem, that he hasn't enough and needs more', in contrast to the rich man, who faces a different problem, as 'many of his desires are no longer even evident to him (unless) nurtured by advertising and salesmanship'.

Our typesetter identifies himself as coming from an 'upper-working-class family', and acknowledges his good fortune in having had a father who was never out of work, and recalls his 'pocket money consisted of a half penny a week, increasing to one penny as we got older. This was spent instantly at the sweet shop. The consequences were that we were unable to get into the shopping mode and found it hard when we finally had money to spend.' He then outlines how, at twelve, he started an evening job and earned 3/6 a week, 'It took me a long time to spend this wisely and at first, I just stowed it away and was slightly scared of touching it. I then got interested in cycling and bought parts for my old bike.' At fourteen he is apprenticed in the printing trade, but does not earn much, while his mates, who are engaged in war work, have higher wages. He then explains, how as 'luxuries were getting scarce', he was finding it

> difficult to compete with them, so even then I really did not get into the shopping habit. My mum still bought my clothes, although I did part with my money for them. I finally snapped out of the doldrums when I discovered girls, for on reflection up to then I had only spent my pocket money on bike parts, youth hostels, picture houses and other odd things. My first real purchase I will always remember, and I was seventeen before this occurred. For weeks I had been looking in Bentall's department store in Kingston at an expensive powder compact my best girlfriend had admired. The shop was eighteen miles away in easy cycling distance, so I visited it a number of times before I plucked up enough courage to part with my hard-earned cash. It was well worth the effort for it was one of the treasures kept for years long after its useful life.

Shopping as narrative: once upon a time . . .

A rich and detailed account, it includes themes which come up in other accounts of shopping for his generation: the connection between earning and spending, the importance of being able to buy sweets for himself, his mother buying his clothes for him, the journey to the shop or store, but also the emotion, in his case love, which took him there, and fixed the memory for him. He is one of the most regular and expressive of the contributors to Mass Observation and the opportunity to tell his tale is also very important to him. It was narrative and the 'intelligible told life' which Alistair MacIntyre (1981) saw as, possibly, offering a way to rescue virtue for a modern world, and it is shopping with its narrative 'quest', journey-like shape and capacity to generate further stories, which makes shopping a culturally rich activity.

For Jerome Bruner (1987, 1990, 1991) narrative is fundamental both to thought, to education and the passing on of values, but also for or to the self, which Bruner sees not as some 'essence to be delved for in the recesses of subjectivity' but the product of 'telling'; and, indeed, argues that the principles of what it is to have a 'self' and to tell a good story are one and the same (Bruner, 2002).We tell stories to be understood, but also to restore a sense of self on the brink of crumbling after the trauma of a nightmare, a birth, getting lost, or just returning from a difficult shopping trip.

Crucially, the stories we tell belong to our culture as much as they do to us and, by telling them, we express our culture as much as we express ourselves. It is a relationship of mutual dependence which Bruner compares to that of the dance and the dancer as neither can exist without the other: the dance needs a dancer to dance it, just as much as the dancer needs a dance to dance. Likewise, culture needs people to express it, by using it, and people need culture to tell their stories so that they will be understood by others. For stories to be told, there have to be people willing and able to tell them, and the right occasion or place for that telling; and traditionally the campfire or the bedtime were such places or occasions. The market, long seen as the hub of social life, is a place for telling and swapping stories, and just as Bassanio and friends would head off to the Rialto for news, whenever they could, so we head off to the shops for news, and return with stories about new stock, or the absence of old stock, of prices, bargains, and special offers. Shopping news is a common currency and if shopping encodes easily into memory because of its narrative shape it is also well remembered because of its capacity to generate stories. Sharon Zukin (2004) describes shopping as a 'talkative practice', and the return from a shopping trip is typically accompanied by a story of how good or bad the parking was, what or who was seen, whether there were crowds, or the place was empty, and whether the trip was a success or a failure.

If a woman is talking to another one about shopping, or about something which either recently purchased, and the other shows interest in the item, or if one woman compliments another on something she has bought or is wearing, that woman is likely to reply, not just with a story about where it came from, how easy or difficult it was to come by, or how much it cost, but also an assessment, if the listener seems interested, of their chances of getting one too. There are many reasons for sharing such information, which is a form of gift, including the norm of reciprocity which requires that something else be given, but also because between women there is what Janet Holmes (1998) calls a strategy of 'positive politeness' used to deflect any envy which might threaten the relationship. Thus the story might start with a disclaimer, for example, 'It was only so much' or 'it is only from. . .'. Telling a story is both an account of a unique experience and a generic one; it may be told as unique, but it will be heard as generic.

Placing something into a recognized pattern makes something more memorable, and the form which shopping takes conforms to the basic rule of all stories, of having a distinct beginning, middle and end, and so it plays out its three acts. The game played with small children which starts 'I went to market and I bought . . .' reinforces the link between shopping, narrative and memory, and it teaches 'shopping talk'. A memory game, in which some things are lost, others are found or added, it encourages what Bruner (2002) calls 'subjunctivizing', the ability to think outside of the box, embellish, deviate, digress, go beyond the given, and see the alternatives. Putting adaptation into a broader perspective, Bruner stresses that humankind is as adapted to culture as to climate or geography, and that this adaptation is achieved through the skill of interpretation and telling stories. One of the themes of this book is that shopping is always about more than buying and is always both a reflection and expression of culture. This can hardly be better illustrated than through the archetypal narrative form of shopping which has all the elements of a story. It takes time, has a destination, an arrival, a series of encounters, of trials, errors, near misses, perhaps a triumph, and then a return. These elements are part of online shopping too, as this involves searching and finding, judgement and comparison, unexpected turns and disappointments and, if shopping on eBay, where timing is critical, real suspense. All of which is as freely talked about to anyone willing to listen, as with any other form of shopping with all the natural embellishments and elaboration.

The story of shopping is told in part because of the traveller's need to tell their tale, to get over it, but also because of lessons to be learned and shared. One of my earliest shopping memories, with all the qualities of the screen memory, is of being told, soon after returning from primary school to put on my coat again for 'we are going out' (the 'we' being my mother, aunt and cousin). So my cousin and I put on our coats and we all walked, for about a mile and a half, in a strange direction. My cousin and I were not told why or where we were going and were puzzled when, arriving at a small shop with high steps, we were asked what we would like to buy? I remember not knowing what this meant, or what there might be to choose from. We had come to a sweet shop on the day that sweets had 'come off the ration' which, across the land, was a major event. I remember I asked my mother to choose for me, but not what she chose, yet to this day I cannot pass that row of shops without wondering which one it was and, if with a companion, telling them about it.

The place of sweetness and light

Personal history and social history always intersect, and reinforcing that particular memory for me is some parallel between the ending of state rationing of sweets and the ending of parental rationing, though in my generation the two are hard to disentangle. For most children, it is a milestone in personal autonomy when they do not have, first, to ask another person it they can have some sweets. Pathetic though it may seem, I can remember this moment very clearly, as I was standing at a bus stop on the embankment, going home in my first year at university, and suddenly realizing that, if I wanted to, I could just go and buy a Mars bar. However, even for those not brought up under austerity, sweets and sweetshops hold a special place in early memories, and a thirty-six year-old warehouseman wrote of how his earliest shopping memory involved

visiting Bennett's shop on the corner of Cauldon Road in Shelton when I was maybe five years old . . . a determinedly old fashioned place with an ancient bacon slicer on the counter and a card of equally venerable pens hanging above the door that gave the shopkeeper access to the living quarters behind his place of business. Best of all, from the perspective of a small boy, was the range of sweets stored in jars on shelves behind the counter. There were more varieties than I could name or have the chance to taste, given three lifetimes in which to tackle the job, though I'd have been more than willing to give it a go had the chance ever presented itself.

Then he adds that another memorable shopping experience from his childhood was the annual visit 'to Bratt and Dyke, a long since vanished department store in Hanley to buy my school uniform. It was an event that marked, through the arrival of another set of scratchy and badly fitting clothes, the official end of the summer holiday, but was thankfully sweetened by a visit to the toy department afterwards.' Not a sweet shop, but note, 'sweetened'.

Sweets are an important part of shopping, whether they are scarce or, as today, can be bought almost anywhere. Sweet shops, though not the consumption of sweets, went into decline, and if the sweet shop is enjoying a revival, this has more to do with the nostalgia for old-fashioned shops than an increase in demand for sweets which rises regardless, sweets being no less desirable now that they are freely available than when they were in short supply. Even so, most children experience something like rationing from their parents, and it is the teasing non-availability of something as desirable as sweets, the ultimate pleasure food, which is hugely significant in childhood, and thus in childhood memories. The pleasure which sweets give, however, is made very complicated by their use as treats, bribes, rewards and, as Isabel Menzies-Lyth (1989) notes, by the primitive fears, fantasies and guilt often associated with pleasure. She further notes that whether sweets are in abundance or not, these very complicated feelings contribute to the frequent complaint made of sweetshops, that 'they never have what you want'.

There are, of course, differences in the experience of shopping today and a couple of generations ago, and the memories of shopping which those who are young today will carry with them are bound to reflect the rise of the supermarket, the expectation of plenty and choice as normal, the availability of many different types of goods in the same place as well as in different places, and, as often as not, of driving rather than walking in order to go shopping. Undergraduate students using the Mass Observation Archive to get 'a feel' of working with primary sources on wartime Britain were surprised to find that in that era people went to different shops for different goods, meat in one shop, bread in another, vegetables in another, and flour or sugar, if you could get it, in yet another. They were also surprised to learn of the 'black market' and the origins of the phrase 'under the counter'. A comparable experience of shopping, which involved subterfuge and circumventing restrictions in the United States would be shopping during the era of Prohibition when the sale of alcohol in the US was banned; children then would have sensed the secrecy associated with its purchase and adults concealing what they were up to. What we take for granted, 'at the time', often seems odd when we step back and look to an era or experience as if we were a stranger or a child. The naming of shops must be as puzzling to small children today as it was in my childhood where some grocers had signs saying 'dry goods', and fish shops were talked about as 'wet fish' shops, but there were no dry ones, though there were fish and chip shops. Some shops were defined as 'hardware' shops, but there were no 'software' shops, and the word 'software', of course, did not then exist. 'Paper' shops sold more than paper, and not only were not all 'corner shops' on corners, not all shops on corners counted as 'corner shops'. Today the equivalent puzzle might be the difference between 'adult' and 'children's shops, though both might sell toys, but of a different type.

The anomalies of shopping classification contribute to making shopping memorable for the children even if it is not until they are much older that they grasp the social meaning of what had perplexed them when young. In my case it was that some butcher shops had signs saying that they were 'Pork Butchers', when it was clear that they sold other sorts of meat too. When I asked my mother, 'Don't all butchers sell pork?' she had no ready explanation, though, after a while, said that pork meant 'quality'. I was unconvinced, for as far as I could see, the butchers all looked alike. It was not until I was much older that I learned that selling pork alongside other meat would make the shop 'unclean' for observant Muslims and Jews, and that dietary laws and prohibitions were important as culture because, by requiring a daily, ritualized observance of difference, they become a daily affirmation of who you were, or were not, which is another example of Mary Douglas's (1997) point about shopping being important as culture because it marks difference. Did my mother know about dietary laws? Probably not, it was just the way it was. And did I remember this occasion because she disappointed me by not having an answer? Perhaps?

In this chapter I have argued that we remember shops and shopping because they are mnemics, because the narrative shape of shopping helps encode the experience of shopping as memory, and because the enclosed shape of the shop allows a certain sort of imaginative freedom, while also containing it, and because many early shopping memories are connected to mother and, also, shame and embarrassment too. However, the shops about which people are often most sentimental are the little ones, the corner shops and village shops, and their dinkyness is a clue to their appeal. In appearance, these shops look more like the toy shops which we may have had as a child than the modern supermarket where, today, much of our daily shopping occurs. The regularity with which toy shops, sweet shops and shoe shops crop up in memories of shopping is no accident, because they most strongly represent our own early life and point of origin. The small size of the shop, and even more the goods they sell, being smaller than us as children, make those goods more manageable and make us, as children, feel bigger, more in control, and more competent. Play shops, like play ironing boards or dolls' houses, require us to act more like grown-ups.

For literary critic Susan Stewart (1984) all distortion, enlargement and miniaturization, is ideological, and she sees the porcelain shepherdesses once very popular with the bourgeoisie as 'erasing' the hard labour which was actually the life of peasants tending sheep, and the small-scale models of the first plant or shop which successful firms often place in their lobbies, as bringing a child-like innocence and authenticity to the version of corporate history which those corporations want to tell, though it may be quite inaccurate. Stewart has a point about distortion, as both enlargement and miniaturization can work commercially: 'bigger' often signals 'better' but small pictures or boxes can often be sold for higher prices than larger items of the same kind, despite lower costs of production, because diminutiveness can also signal preciousness. Little shops, and the 'boutique' in particular, have bucked some of the trend towards larger chain stores and department stores, and while they may not have held their own in the high street, the boutique has reappeared inside the larger stores as 'franchises'.

Scale matters both psychologically and symbolically, and the small shops figure in memory as much as they do, partly because shops retain an element of the toyshop, the sweet shop and the shoe shop. In the next chapter we will see more of how shopping can encourage growth, but to conclude this one I want to take the account of growth given by the narrator in Philip Roth's (2006) novel *Everyman*, whom we meet at his father's funeral where he is reflecting on both his own and his father's life. We learn of how father had opened a small jewellery store, and taken on the risks of self employment when his second son, the narrator, was born, so that there would be 'something to leave his two boys'. We learn, too, that at the age of seventy-three the father sold the store, 'having by then sold engagement and wedding rings to three generations of Elizabeth families'. The store is described as the embodiment of hard work, trust and virtue, as lives inside the store mirrored those outside, and the narrator recalls how:

> Over the years our father sold wedding rings to Elizabeth's Irish and Germans and Slovaks and Italians and Poles, most of them young working-class stiffs. Half the time, after he'd made the sale, we'd be invited, the whole family, to the wedding . . . He never checked their credit (and) never went broke with their credit, the goodwill generated by his flexibility was more than worth it . . . and at Christmastime he always had a snow scene with Santa in the window.' But the stroke of genius, we are told, was the father's decision 'to call the business not by his name, but rather Everyman's Jewelry Store.

The father had taught his sons many lessons, including that 'It's a big deal for working people to buy a diamond, no matter how small. The wife can wear it for the beauty and she can wear it for the status. And when she does, this guy is not just a plumber – he's a man with a wife with a diamond.' Then the narrator tells of how as a child he had 'loved being only nine years old and carrying the diamonds in an envelope in his jacket pocket onto the bus to Newark, where the setter and the sizer and the polisher and the watch repairman our father used each sat in a cubbyhole of his own . . . Those trips gave that kid enormous pleasure. I think watching those artisans doing their lonely work in those tight little places gave him the idea for using his hands to make art.' The setters, sizers and polishers were not toy men, and their cubbyholes not toy shops, but it was their smallness which, as miniatures, appears to have helped the boy locate a version of a self, and a future. The jewellery shop was the narrator's point of origin, memory and imagination, and it was the tiny cubby holes in which the sizers and setters sat which 'subjunctivized' him. Subjunctivizing is not how we normally think of education, or shopping, but shopping is about learning and it helps us grow up, not just once, but again and again as we progress through the life course, which is the subject of the next chapter.

4

Signposts and Shopping Milestones: Too Old for Topshop?

Children may not be 'born to shop', but shopping defines us in our passage through life and nudges us along the life course. From the first solo trip to the shops which is a test of trust and physical competence to the last, shopping is sewn into our lives, mirroring our progress, marking transitions. Buying the first school uniform, the first bra or the first pair of high heels (red in my case), a first suit, or a first layette for the first grandchild, all these mark stages of life as much as the first day at school or college. However, it is not just the products which are symbolic, the first pen or watch which tell the world that we can now write and tell the time, it is also the process of buying or receiving which makes us feel more grown up. The first time we are allowed to choose our own clothes, or are 'fitted' for shoes, a bra, or, for a boy, a suit, while an often unnerving ritual, can make a child feel more grownup, important and substantial. Of course, at root it is biology which pushes us along the life course and into the shops, for just as children grow out of shoes and clothes, and need new ones, so too do adults, as their girths and necks widen or shrink and they discover that they have grown out of clothes before the clothes have worn out. But ageing is not just biology, it is also social, and sometimes we buy new clothes because we know that the old ones are just not suitable for the age that we now are.

Happy birthday tomorrow

The age which we feel ourselves to be is not always, and for some of us, perhaps, never, the same as the one on our birth certificate, and at different points in our life shopping will highlight this. It does it most obviously through the signs in stores which sell alcohol and/or cigarettes warning customers, very nicely, that they might be asked to show identification, or which simply enquire 'Under 25?' Baby clothes are marked quite precisely in terms of age: 0–3 months, 3–6 months, 6–12 months, and so on up to about eighteen months, when age begins to give way to size. There are children's clothes shops, and in some richer areas, school uniform shops too, then there are teenage accessory shops, but soon after the early teen years age goes underground, and gives way to stage which is registered with bridalwear shops, then babywear shops, etc. and the whole cycle starts again. Some man-ufacturers, and stores, have special lines which fairly clearly signal different age groups. Marks and Spencer, for example, includes in its womenswear ranges, 'Classics' for the older customer, while 'Per Una' is for twenty to thirty year olds, and older women too who still want to look pretty. 'Limited Collection' is for the more fashionable, and a slightly more upmarket 'Autograph' is for 'forty somethings' who want to pass for thirty-five, and then there is 'Portfolio' for older women who want to look something other than a 'typical Granny'. The high street, or main street, may stalk us, but it also talks to us, and cues us into making the next step in life. In a skit about feeling one's age, the persona, 'Lily Savage', created by comedian Paul O'Grady, illustrated this with the quip that 'you know you are getting old when, on walking through a Marks and Spencer store, you hear yourself say: "Now, there's a nice pair of slacks."' Or, as happened to a petite friend, the moment came when even she was too old for Topshop.

Age and stage of life are not the same, but both affect how we shop, and this chapter is about the central, unrealized role which shops and shopping play in our growing up and growing old. We are shoppers before we are workers, and we continue as shoppers, often more avidly, when we retire. The 'pocket money' given to us so that we can learn 'the value of money' is spent in shops, and shops are also where we practise the small civilities of everyday life such as saying 'please' and 'thank you', of waiting patiently, of opening doors and letting others pass, returning things to where we found them, and refraining from pushing and shoving. As we get older, we learn when or not to make eye or body contact in shops, especially in changing rooms; and we learn about shopping in school as part of personal and social education (PSE) or 'Citizenship'. If we learn a foreign language one of the first exercises will be learning how to ask for food, drink, water, petrol or stamps in a shop, the most basic skill needed for survival when abroad. Shopping is a life skill and being 'good at shopping' may, during the testing school years when being 'good at something' is critical, be life saving. Our first job is likely to be in a shop on a Saturday, and, like all other 'firsts', the first love, or the first shopping trip as a couple, it will have a profound and lasting effect. For someone only recently a teenager, realizing that they are now old enough to make use of a tie pin or pair of cufflinks can be a shock, while at the end of a working life, knowing that one no longer has any need for a suit can offer the exquisite pleasure of walking straight past that section of a store. Finally, when we can no longer shop for ourselves, and have to depend on others to shop for us, or to drive us to the shops, this marks our decline as powerfully as having to leave our own home. A milestone for us, it is also a milestone for the rest of our family too. Though younger folk often attempt to pass as older than they really are, the goal for older folk is more often to look younger and most women of a certain age walk a tightrope in their efforts neither to look their age, nor appear as 'mutton dressed as lamb'. However, many older people of both sexes are very proud of not looking or feeling old and, as historian Paul Thompson (1990) found, would not, as a matter of self respect, shop in 'old people's shops'.

Reading, writing and reacting

Of course, this will be different in different cultures, but the more 'retailized' the society, the greater will be the part played by shops and shopping in equipping individuals, cognitively, emotionally and socially, to 'fit in'. Shops are where we practice our newly learned skills of reading, writing and arithmetic and, in later life, they are where we keep them 'functional'. The activity of shopping requires us to read labels and directions, perhaps to compose a shopping list, to compare and work out unit prices, to check change, understand technical and nutritional information, and generally organize ourselves. Almost any child of the twentieth century born before the era of the supermarket will have learned something about classification as they moved, with their mother, from shop to shop, each selling a different class of goods. They would have learned that meat comes from butchers, some of whom are also 'pork' butchers, that there are bakers who bake only bread, and others who bake cakes and pastries too, green grocers and ordinary grocers, wet fish shops and dry goods shops, men's shops and women's shops, and they would have garnered a familiarity with systems of classification which are the building block of all organized thought.

The lessons of life are learned in many ways, and in many contexts, and, of course, occur not only in childhood. Some of the skills which would ideally be learned in childhood and are not, may be acquired later on, without any further formal education. In a study of adults who had failed miserably at school to grasp any of the principles of mathematics, but could nevertheless use mathematical knowledge very effectively when shopping for groceries in a supermarket, cognitive anthropologist Jean Lave (1988, 1996) showed that learning was not a process confined to, or contained in, the mind of the learner, and that the context was an integral aspect of the activity. Lave reasoned that while the mind might be *in* the individual, the mind was developed *in* social situations, and that a person will use whatever is to hand in the way of tools or circumstances to support and 're-organize mental functioning'. Mathematical knowledge is, perhaps, an especially abstract form of knowledge, and might be thought to be context-free. Yet, quite the opposite, for as Lave showed, it was extremely context-dependent. In her study the supermarket could 'call forth' the ability to use mathematical principles, where the school, designed for that purpose had failed. The lesson Lave takes from this is that learning is 'a flexible process of engagement with the world', and part of what she calls a 'community of practice'. Educationalists have long talked of 'informal learning', but Lave's focus was specifically on the setting being as dynamic and as changeable as the person engaging with it. Calculating a 'best buy' in a supermarket was not a 'bounded' or self contained activity, and was influenced by other activities which might be going on at the same time, and by aspects of the setting such as large signs suggesting special 'offers' and 'deals', which could lead a person to change their mind or priorities.

Lave's approach was a challenge to conventional theories of learning which see learning as a process which goes on almost singularly in the mind. Her work, unusual in her field, broke down the idea of there being a firm boundary between an activity and its setting, which is why she used the terms 'situated action' or 'situated learning', 'community of practice' and 'knowledgeability'. In other fields, however, this boundary has not been not been conceived of quite so firmly. For example, in Donald Winnicott's (1971) approach to human development, where the mother is 'the environment', it is crucial that the boundary between mother and infant be very permeable, as this enables the competence and understanding of the mother to be transferred to the child. Ideally, the mother is so 'attuned' to her child that she knows what it wants almost before it does, and can provide it. In the longer run this lays the basis for the ability to feel, and be, creative. It is an illusion, but if the infant can imagine that it has created what it wants or needs it will feel powerful and that helps the infant to become so. The parallels with retail and businesses serving the mass market are clear enough: they have to anticipate demand and, in fashion especially, producers and retailers need to be several seasons ahead as the goods have to be in the shops, available, when the customers want them. In the increasing focus given today on service and 'staying close to the customer' or, as Paul du Gay (1996) prefers, 'making up' the customer, the training of staff to identify with customers as individuals having the same sorts of needs, wants and desires as themselves, we can see a version of this 'attunement', though Du Gay sees it as a form of 'Foucauldian' social control. In his critique of life under 'late modernity' Ian Craib (1994) suggests that people have become 'ill-equipped to bear much disappointment'. As a result, they have developed a characteristically impatient 'false self' which renders them unable to stand back from 'the desire for narcissistic gratification', so that they revert quickly to the aggressive defences of infancy. However there is nothing regressive or infantile about finding a skirt, pair of boots, book or computer which are 'just right', or 'just what I wanted', or in finding that every season the high street hits the right note at the right moment.

Backstage: the eight ages of man

Early life, and childhood experience in general, continue to affect us throughout our lives, and though we, in a sense, 'pass through' the various stages of growth, and more or less surmount the challenges which each stage presents to us, the distinctive states of mind associated with those stages remain part of our emotional 'repertoire'. These states of mind can then be re-experienced in later life if circumstances arise which evoke the same sort of feelings as those we experienced at an earlier stage in life. Shopping, too, presents its challenges, and to illustrate how these may be experienced, as versions of earlier challenges, it is useful to take the eight-stage model of development offered by Erik Erikson (1950) focusing, as Erikson does, more on the fifth stage, adolescence, than on the other stages. Erikson's approach is psychodynamic, and the processes which he is discussing are unconscious, as are the associations connected to them, which I am suggesting give some pattern to some of our shopping behaviour or style.

The model is based on the premise that each stage is defined by a particular task which, if successfully mastered, leads to growth and integration, both physical and psychological, but which, if not successfully met, stunts development. The model is chronological, so it implies that people move on and pass through the stage, more or less successfully. Which, of course, we all do, to a degree. But the past is never wholly left behind and we carry the experience of each stage, unconsciously, as a 'feeling'. The feelings which we have about shopping, the goods we buy, and the shops, or any other mode of buying, are sourced in earlier experience, just as are many other feelings we have about various activities, people or things.

The primary task of the first stage, in Erikson's model, is to learn how to feed successfully, and this requires that the infant can trust the person caring for them. If they do, and everything goes well, that infant is more likely to become a generally trusting person; but if it does not go well, then the infant is likely to become generally wary, suspicious and untrusting. Applied to shopping this might explain why for some people shopping is always disappointing and shops places where 'you never get what you want' and must vigilantly check change because you will probably be cheated. The solution for such people might appear to be, for them, to avoid shopping and to opt for the most impersonal forms, such as mail order or the internet. For other people, shops are fondly remembered as places run by nice folk, who knew your name and gave you sweets, and for such people shopping continues to be agreeable. The primary tasks of the second and third stages, toilet training and establishing independence by walking, holding, touching, grasping and all the other exploratory behaviour typical of toddlerdom, smelling, prodding and testing are all easily and frequently done in shops, and from being sat in a supermarket trolley. Feeling, touching, assessing and choosing, are also the prototype experiences needed to become a good shopper as an adult. Becoming more assertive and independent is part of the challenge of these stages and though, if practiced in shops by toddlers, can lead to chastisement and, perhaps, feelings of failure and shame, shopping can contribute to quite important developmental shifts. A key moment in cognitive development is the ability to reverse a situation and see it from another angle, and a quite testing situation for the young child is grasping the concept of 'change' and that the shopkeeper or assistant does not give you both goods and money.

The fourth stage, latency, is typified by an obsessive learning style based on amassing information and collecting; traditionally this involved postage stamps or bird's eggs, though today it is more likely to be Dr Who cards and football regalia; but it may also coincide with beginning to take an interest in shopping. This can come on quite suddenly and replace some other previously absorbing activity, say, horse riding, which is dropped in favour of shopping on a Saturday morning with friends. Growing up, becoming more independent, learning things for yourself, rather than being taught them also means detaching yourself from parents, and finding a place within a peer group, and not just a social place, but a physical one too. As places in which to work and buy, shops serve these needs for both sexes, as boys use malls, shops and stores to build friendship and competence just as much as do girls. The importance of peers in latency and adolescence is linked to the growing importance of personal identity which, in turn, is linked to who your friends are, and shopping can be a way of sorting this out. A student of mine once bravely described how it had become a custom among her friends to prepare for a day in town by squashing into a photo-booth for a group photo of the 'in group'. Equipped with multiple copies of this picture, with its sticky back, they would leave a trail of them in the changing rooms, toilets and other parts of stores where they would be found by other girls, who would know, then, that they had been left out. The developmental 'task' then absorbing the group was learning how to manage the tension between their destructive and constructive impulses, and how to exert control and mastery while allowing others to do likewise. The girls' choice of the high street suggests a connection between their internal worlds full of greed and envy and the shops overflowing with goods which they could not have. Wanting to attack things which you desire but which are unavailable is normal, and the girls' behaviour, cruel as it was, can be seen as them, unconsciously, displacing their frustration by attacking through excluding another group of girls. The girls were acting as a gang, and the point of a 'gang mentality' is to relieve the individual of responsibility for their own feelings and channel them instead through the group (see Waddell, 1998). Of course, any interpretation, from a distance, is speculative, but the shock expressed by the student as she realized what they had done, and as she was describing it, was very real.

The fifth stage of life, adolescence, is a period when the inner world is classically in turmoil and the main task is that of sorting out identity, politics, careers and sexuality, so it is no wonder that adolescents flock to malls as places where they can try on, or try out, different versions of themselves, as well as test the boundaries set by the adult world. A shoplifting expedition is almost an adolescent rite of passage and, in his autobiography, actor and writer Stephen Fry (1997) describes his experiment at pilfering from the shop nearest to his much-hated school as a dry run for a later criminal act which he hoped would, as it did, get him expelled. Another man, now a successful businessman, recalled how his singular try at shoplifting coincided with realizing that his mother did not automatically know what he was up to wherever he was and at any time. Still, he took care to conduct his experiment in the nearby town and not the one in which they lived. Growing up means distancing yourself from your parents and, for a time, this often involves rejecting many of things associated with them, including the shops the parents choose to use. Many teenagers simply refuse to step inside certain stores, especially well-known ones which they see as middle aged and middle class. Though, as the younger generation move through the life course, they often find their way back to those very same stores and even congratulate themselves on having 'discovered' them.

Finding our way to shops, or back to shops, is a re-tracing of our own life course and, though, in practical terms, much of the shopping we do is done for other people, as most of it is done alone, it brings up or brings out something quite narcissistic, which is exquisitely captured in the Eudora Welty (1979) tale of 'The Little Store' which opens with a mother's call for someone to run to the neighbourhood shop for her, and the child, her daughter, eagerly responds. Full of a child's sense of being at the centre of the world, the story examines this up to the child's loss of narcissistic innocence in one shocking revelation about the real world. The journey is described as the girl knowing the way to the store 'as well as she knew her own skin', and omnipotently peopled in her head with a kaleidoscope of possible encounters, adventures and memories. On arrival, Welty describes the store as displaying a feast of sights and sensations which existed just for the little girl: kerosene, molasses, matches, vinegar, starch, spinning tops, sardines, salt and harmonicas, waiting for her, and the shopkeeper, too, who exists to fuss over her and measure how much she has grown. 'Setting out in this world' Welty writes, 'a child feels so indelible' and 'only comes to find out later that it's all the others along the way who are making themselves indelible to him'. The child, now grown, Welty continues, still cannot 'to this day . . . picture the store with a grown person in it . . . We children thought it was ours. The happiness of errands was in part that of running for the moment away from home . . . But the day came when I ran to the store to discover. . .'. The family had disappeared. The little girl never learns why, but she had flashes of memory of little things relating to the store, which were odd and out of place, the sudden and untimely appearance of the 'Monkey Man'. There is no suggestion in the story that the girl herself suffered some trauma, but the description is similar to a dislocated 'screen memory', and the point of the story is of some experience too awful to really know about, and to show how the girl comes to realize that life was more complex than running errands and being full of herself. Welty gets into the child's latency related obsession with collecting and memorizing as she walks along to the little store, and thinks of all the children and adults that she had ever passed on her way to it: all her adventures, all the goods stocked, the owner who weighed her on his scales, set her subtractions, and tolerated the time it took her to decide how to spend her nickel reward for running the errand. 'Everyone I saw on my way seemed to me then part of my errand, and in a way they were . . . All the years we lived in that house where we children were born, the same people lived in the other houses on our street too. People changed through the arithmetic of birth, marriage and death, but not by going away. So families just accrued stories, which through the fullness of time, in those times, their own lives made.' My précis does not do justice to the elegance and sensitivity of Welty's prose, or the picture she gives of an innocent self centredness which remains part of the way we shop for all of us, and which is not reprehensible, but is important to acknowledge.

Compared to the earlier stages in Erikson's account the later ones are more compressed, but the developmental tasks and challenges of early adulthood, namely, of establishing intimacy, finding a partner and suitable work are all reflected in shopping style. With two incomes, and before children come along, shopping can be part of a new intimacy, but later this becomes less likely. The middle years of adult life, focused on building a family and career, supporting the next generation, and perhaps the older one too, lead to different sorts of shopping, the out-of-town retail park rather than the high street or specialist shop, and to shopping with children or older parents, rather than as a couple. Various changes in family life impact on shopping most obviously, of course, the arrival of children, and the early years of parenthood generally squeeze out most 'personal shopping', leaving mostly general provisioning and caring. If the children turn out to be 'fussy eaters' and/or need special diets then provisioning can become very complicated and time consuming (see De Vault, 1994). In the final stage, reflecting on, viewing and accommodating to what has been, the ability to still shop for yourself is not only a matter of self respect, but is a measure of competence used in assessing eligibility for various forms of state assistance. Completing the cycle, the sweets which were important in childhood tend to become so again in old age and as we move through the life course the shopping which perhaps means most to us moves from sweets to shopping for clothes and then back to sweets.

Trust me: red apple, green apple

However, as striking as the fit between how shopping changes over a lifetime and Erikson's scheme, is that the same issues of trust, safety, autonomy, initiative and independence which thread through Erikson's early stages are repeated in the history of shops and shopping. Initially, traders were pedlars and strangers who could not be trusted and, with both buyer and seller suspicious of the other, each would bargain hard. But when shops became permanent establishments with fixed prices and purchasing was often done daily, traders became neighbours, and relations between them began to mellow, loyalties were established and personal favours, like credit, which depend on trust, more routine. Later, as the scale of commercial enterprise grew, and the personal basis of trust was replaced by impersonal legislation, protection for customers was generalized, rather than depending on establishing a special relationship. Government, unions, and charities began to be concerned about the conditions suffered by shop workers, as well as the interests of traders and consumers, and regulations were introduced covering trading and working hours, labour conditions, as well as standards, prices, measures, weights, ingredients, and, latterly health and safety (see Hilton, 2003). Traders, increasingly mindful of their good reputations, could no longer afford to see what they could get away with, and faulty goods became the exception rather than the rule. Responsibility rested with the trader, not the producer, and sensible arrangements for returning goods gradually became commonplace. Customer protection has now spread beyond the economic to the physical, with CCTV and security guards installed to deter shoplifting; however, though these give some customers a sense of greater security, they increase a sense of insecurity for others, if they fear being suspected as a potential shoplifter.

Consumer associations, newspaper consumer columns and the web, where consumer feedback has become part of the regulatory framework, have added to a sense of consumer rights, while branding has built, and largely delivered, confidence in products as reliable, safe, known and understood. Shopping can still be felt as risky, and the pushing of store cards, deals and credit is perhaps the modern equivalent of shaved coins. But the reduction in risk, both in relation to shopping, and life more generally, has been accompanied by an increased fear of risk, something which can hardly be more clearly demonstrated than by the contemporary shock reaction to leaving babies unattended in prams outside shops, common practice only a generation or two ago. The risks of buying are different but, as this brief account of shopping history shows, the general trend has been away from risk and towards safety and protection, a shift which increases both the resonance of shopping today with early life as safe and customer expectations of ultra-tolerant, caring and parent-like treatment from shops and their staff. We are often very narcissistic when it comes to shopping, or what Thomas Hine (2002) calls the 'buyosphere', the whole conglomeration of physical and virtual places, and a state of mind, which Hine sees as 'our chief arena of expression, the place where we learn most about who we are, both as people and as individuals'.

Different again: . . . said Alice

Life is a progression, socially, culturally and developmentally, and one which is required both by culture and family life to be marked by giving gifts. Aged nineteen, and one year out of school, my daughter felt herself to be quite a different person to the one which she had been a year earlier, and at twenty-two, and a year out of university, she felt different again. In order to get a tenancy, she had had to present herself as a 'young profes-sional', and almost immediately she suggested that from now on 'homeware' would make good Christmas or birthday presents for her. Most birthdays, especially the 'big ones', of the first birthday, the eighteenth or twenty-first, the fiftieth and the hundredth, as well as all the others in between, are occasions for giving gifts; and the gift market is a major part of the economy, certainly of the retail sector. Gifts are given to mark the transition of stage of life as well as of age, so, classically, a ring is given by a man to a woman on getting engaged and then another ring is given at the wedding, and traditionally, as gifts from others, most of what would be needed to set up home. Gifts are also given, sometimes, at graduation, when leaving a job or retiring from one, as well as on other anniversaries such as a first date, or, later, silver, golden, diamond and ruby weddings. Gifts are also given for personal achievements; perhaps, for example, for someone who had found learning to drive very difficult. Almost all of these gifts are bought rather than made, so someone has to find and buy them. Giving a voucher, rather than the thought, 'which counts', is usually viewed as somewhat feeble, and means that the value of a gift is diminished because the thought and the leg work is transferred to the recipient. Though in scale, gift buying may not be the larger part of our annual shopping, in terms of thought given to finding 'the right gift', or agonizing about it, it is a highly significant part of our shopping. Still, it is not only through the giving and receiving of gifts that shopping contributes to moving from one stage of life to another stage, shops are the stages on which we do some of our growing up.

In another short story, Mary Gordon's (2006) 'Now I am Married', a newly wed second wife is followed on a first testing visit to her new English in-laws as she buys the ingredients for a ratatouille. 'This morning', reflects the new wife,

> I took my sister-in-law's basket and went out, married, to the market. I don't think that marriage has changed me, but for the first time, the salespeople appreciated, rather than resented, the time I took choosing only the most heart-warming tomatoes, the most earnest and forthright meat. I was no longer a fussy bachelorette who cooked only sometimes and at her whim. I was a young matron in stockings and high heels. My selections, to them, had something to do with the history they were used to. They were important not for myself. I had wanted to write this morning, but I had the responsibility of dinner, served at one. I do not say this in complaint. I was quite purely happy with my basket and my ring, basking in the approval of the shop-keepers and the pedestrians.

Now a wife with a new role, the woman feels that she fits in better and is integrated by her performance of shopping for others, and she feels duly rewarded with approval. Her change of personal status changes the meaning of shopping. As both public and private places, shops are often used to display and enact the new roles which come with new relationships, for example, the public performance of a private 'togetherness' by a young couple in a supermarket which gave Daniel Miller (1998) his chapter title 'Making Love in Supermarkets'.

The meaning of shopping changes because family life changes, as families have a life course too. Children grow up and leave home, partners die and or leave home too, sometimes adult children return, and each time shopping changes. Buying for one, after fifty years of buying for two, or five, can be a piercing daily reminder of loss. When my mother was widowed she would often say that what she missed most was 'having someone to buy shirts for', and though

I was unsure how much it was the 'someone' or the 'shopping' which was most missed, either way, it was clear that the task had kept alive the sense of being in a relationship and of being a wife, not a widow. As a wife, my mother felt that she had the right to be in the menswear department, something which was important to her as, by profession, she was a tailor and wanted to keep a hold on that world too. Of course, there was no sign saying 'widows and single women keep out', but she felt out of place and imagined that the shop assistants knew she was a widow. Daniel Miller and Fiona Parrott (2009) make the same point in an article on loss and material culture when pointing out that most purchases are driven by an attempt to close the gap between how the actual person or relationship really is, or was, and the idealized version of that. Even without bereavement, shopping changes with age and retirement, for example, men who had previously regarded shopping as a tiresome and trivial occupation sometimes start to take an interest in it, though not always to the delight of their wives whose hearts sink on hearing those five little words, 'Shall I come with you?'

Shopping, which brings into question the status of our family life and relationships, is also used to a way of improving or sustaining relationships, whether or not it is done as a shared activity. The example given in the last chapter of how shopping became almost the only activity Linda Grant could still do with her mother, in her last years, and how much it was appreciated by both women because it made sense of their relationship and brought intimacy and connection back into it, illustrates the broader theme that shopping is deeply embedded in relationships. Making the same point in a study of men in same-sex couple households, Christopher Carrington (2002) shows how the partner who becomes the 'consumption specialist' often uses everyday shopping as an opportunity to think about relationships and build family and relational solidarity by thinking about possible presents for their partner, or their wider family. The same study also showed how the purchase of consumer durables was linked symbolically to ideas of stability in the relationship, and to its prospects of durability. However, neither relationships, nor the life course, are quite as durable as once they were and in the richer nations, age and stage of life have become increasingly de-coupled. The age and order in which people marry, have children, leave home, set up their own home, go to university, graduate, start work, or leave it, have become more scrambled. Culture still gives people an idea about the shape which life might be expected to take, but in practice these stages have become less predictable or, as Elizabeth Beck-Gernsheim (1998) puts it, more 'elective'.

The high street has kept up with this particular social change and, while traditionally progression through the life course was clearly inscribed in the high street or main street: with one shop for the school uniform, one for the first suit or overall, another for the wedding dress, and yet another for the layette, this is no the longer the case, and most of these goods can now be found under one roof in a supermarket. Judging by the disappearance of the wedding gift department from department stores, and its replacement by the all-purpose gift shop, or gift department, the high street is very much in touch with the time. Cohabitees are generally not given presents when they set up home, but the high street continues energetically to promote St Valentine's Day, and imaginatively to create further occasions for a ritualized giving of gifts. As populations have become richer, their lives longer and more varied, more moments appear worthy of marking with gifts. Though not all are quite the milestones of birthdays, wedding anniversaries and retirement, many are life stages and are marked with gifts which someone has bought. The high street which has adapted well to change in patterns of personal life, and is discreet about the biology of ageing, has swiftly adapted to this; so Tesco-online sends congratulations to customers who have just added newborn size nappies to their regular order, and mail promoting hearing aids, bathroom aids, stair lifts and Saga holidays will start to pour through the letterbox as soon as you turn fifty.

The high street: a grey area

In almost all the richer nations pensioners now outnumber children and though, in theory, the 'grey pound', 'grey dollar' and 'grey vote' are well understood, you would not know this from a walk down the high street where the message is that the shopper is forever young. There are no old people in the shop windows and no 'senior' departments, as there are 'children's departments' though there are plenty of old people on the pavements. Though in some parts of the United States, where winters are very harsh, mall-walking has been developed as a way for older people to keep fit, old people are mostly invisible in the high street, not physically, but symbolically. Some shops clearly cater for the older age group and sell walking sticks, thermal underwear and hearing aids, and there are others, which are rather unstylish and known as 'Granny shops' by the young who, unless they have found a job in one, avoid them. Ageing had not been abolished, and most sixty-year-old women are not trying to have babies, but ageing has come to be seen almost as voluntary, and phrases such as 'sixty is the new forty', though mainly said ironically, are also signs of the social pressure to deny the march of biology. Ambivalence is the most striking feature of our relationship to looking or feeling old and the high street captures this precisely. For, while privately fuming at the difficulty of finding clothes in larger sizes or 'interesting' colours which, unfairly as it seems to some, are kept only in smaller sizes, many people do not want to be consigned to buying their clothes at a shop which specializes in 'outsize' garments. We are often revealed to ourselves by shopping, finding that we are not the size which we thought we were, because shops mirror us, literally, and show us aspects of ourselves, our squatness or greyness, which we would rather not see. Thus, when a shop such as the Dutch clothing chain C&A, a long-term fixture in the British high street too, much depended upon for larger sizes, announced that it was pulling out, there was a panicked rush to buy from it before it was too late. Likewise, the disappearance of downtown department stores in the U.S, and the 'boutique-ization' of those which remain, has similarly scrambled the mental 'road map' of older shoppers.

Kathleen Woodward (1991) describes the invisibility of old age as one of its 'discontents', and the marked invisibility of old age in the high street may be openly explained because old age is not attractive, commercially, or personally, except for anti-ageing products. Many of the products bought by older people, for example, support stockings, hair dye or Viagra, do not lend themselves to a 'good' display and, as often also linked to physical disability they are sold discreetly, and in more 'hidden ways, such as through small ads, mail order or online, in order not to draw attention. Though size is a major problem for older people buying clothes, it is not only a problem for older people, as a young person suffering from a condition which makes them overweight, such as Prader-Willi syndrome, having to buy clothes in an 'outsize' shop is devastating. It was equally embarrassing for a man, always on the short side, but who had shrunk further with age, to find that after failing to buy a pair of plain grey trousers from the usual sources, he was driven to buying them from a school uniform shop amid privately educated teenage boys and their mothers. However this is not an issue which gets much attention until it happens to you, or someone in your family, when stores that had long been relied upon, such as C&A or Marks and Spencer, seem to 'let you down'. As one woman, writing for Mass-Observation observed, this was a bit of a shock. 'Always a fan of M&S' she says,

> I have been disappointed for some time because I have been unable to stock my wardrobe from its rails. At first I thought it was my age and that as I grew older I perhaps should not expect to be able to shop as I did previously. Then I remembered that my mother had always shopped there for her classical shirt-waisters and suchlike until she was much older than I am. We all seemed to shop there regardless of our age.

Regardless of age, or regardless of fashion; and what does it mean to be too old for Topshop? If the high street discriminates against old age it is because fashion discriminates: the shirtwaister was never fashionable and when it was reliably available was when fashion was just one sector of the rag trade, along with workwear, children's wear and menswear etc. Then it was fashion which was exceptional, and fashion wear was signalled by shop signs, as in 'ladies fashions' rather than 'ladies' or 'women's' wear. There are, of course, many factors behind this change; globalization, which has made clothes much cheaper, the cheap end of the market as fashion conscious as the high end, and spread fashion beyond clothing to other goods, is the most obvious. Also important is that much less of the work done in the post-industrial world is dirty, heavy work, and much less of it is uniformed work, which means that more people are free, within limits, to choose what they wear to work. Armed with that choice and, as fashion is about wearing clothes which are both aesthetically pleasing and sexually attractive, more people wear more fashionable clothes, at least if they are young. However, once past the reproductive years, men and women tend to look more alike, as both sexes get grey hair and rounder, and their attire becomes blander and more unisex; not just because they have lost interest but because the market has no interest in them. Diana Crane (2000) reports that American market-research analysts split the clothing market into three major groups: women under twenty-five, and particularly under twenty, women of twenty-five and over, and affluent women between thirty-five and fifty. They know that the average American woman is over forty, and possibly quite well off, but do not cater for them, and believe that this group spends less money on clothes because they are more interested in other activities. Chicken or egg? This book has not been about fashion, but fashion obviously influences shopping and is part of the reason older shoppers feel let down or ignored by the high street/main street. Crane concludes that 'fashion's social agenda always speak to and for certain social groups, and exclude others' and, while in the nineteenth century those excluded were of 'inferior social status', or anyone unwilling or unable to conform to a specific gender ideal, in the late twentieth century exclusion was more likely to be based on age, and sometimes race. Older shoppers do sometimes benefit from the greater focus on younger shoppers and, as Paco Underhill (1999) reports, the two demographic groups that together make up the major part of the market for 'trainer' shoes, are teenagers and men over sixty. There are some signs of the high street responding to the 'grey' pound or dollar, as more stores provide chairs and sofas, and those which closed their restrooms and restaurants are re-instating them. In Germany, where one in three people are now over the age of fifty, a Senioren Supermarkt with wide aisles, large price tags, hanging magnifying glasses and trolleys which transform into chairs was piloted in Berlin, and it would interesting to know if that had been a success. However, the story told by the shopping mall or main street, remains one of eternal youth.

5

Shopping: A Rough Guide to Gender

'Western Women's Clothing: sizes 8–30.'

Shop Sign, London, NW1

Of all the social distinctions which cultures worldwide mark and require their members to observe, the social difference between men and women is the most vital. How it is marked, physically, through segregation, or expressively, through language, dress and demeanour will vary, but that it is marked will not. The question for this chapter is not why gender differences exist in any society, but how shopping contributes to that difference. In traditional cultures where, by custom or religion, women live more secluded lives than men, or very remote rural areas where buying anything involves a long and possibly risky journey, shopping is an activity mostly reserved for men. In parts of Nepal, for example, men take on shopping as part of seeking paid work away from home, as this gets them both cash and nearer to places where they can spend it. In other places, not so poor or traditional, women do all, or most, of the shopping, though rarely for as practical a reason as that given in Nepal for women not doing it. The reasons given for the sexual division of labour, in whatever form it takes, are not always consistent. Because shopping is often seen as part of housework, and as moderately combinable with childcare, in some places childcare is given as the reason why women do most shopping, but in other places childcare is given as the reason for women not shopping. The detail does not matter, as the point, for culture, is simply that gender is marked, and any sexual division of labour will suffice.

All societies have some system, 'order' or 'regime', which governs how work, power, emotion and care-taking are divided along the lines of gender, and in many cultures language is gendered too. This is not so with the English language, and in English-speaking communities it is possibly harder to realize that gender is not only an attribute of living creatures, but also of goods, houses, ships, shops and most of the activities associated with them too. Both degree and manner of marking gender varies, and is achieved not only by separation or segregation, but also by approach or attitude. In most societies there are many tasks and activities which are undertaken by both sexes, but towards which each sex tends to take a somewhat different approach. Shopping is one such example, and driving, perhaps, another. Though he sees women becoming more like men in the way that they shop, Paco Underhill (1999) does not see them, at least not yet, as the impatient 'loose cannons' he dubs men, nor does he include women in his advice to retailers to make shopping more like driving if they want it to appeal more to men. Gender differentiates, and so does shopping. Where shopping is an activity done by both sexes, and even, sometimes, together, the difficulties commonly experienced by heterosexual couples are the result of the different gendered 'ways of seeing things'. So, while a wife or girlfriend might despair at her partner for buying the first thing he sees, he might be delighted at having achieved his shopping goal very quickly. This is maybe a stereotype, and there are plenty of exceptions, especially among younger men. But stereotypes play an important role in culture as 'rough guides', and it is as crucial for culture that they exist for us to use, as it is for us to have some idea of how to behave as a man or woman should in our society, and how to understand the behaviour of others.

We learn about gendered behaviour, and how to 'do' it, in many settings, at home, school, in the street, and when we go shopping. The idea that gender is something which we 'do' rather than 'have', as part of ourselves, like a trait, was the insight of sociologists

Candace West and Don Zimmerman (1987), and it changed how gender was thought about. Rather than treating gender as mainly the result of childhood socialization and rather like an inoculation which, once given, lasted for life, West and Zimmerman's approach stressed that gender had to be performed, and with this made gender more reflexive, interactive and interesting. We express, signal or 'do' gender in the way we walk, talk, dress and hold ourselves, in the way we behave differently in the company of our own or the opposite sex, and the way we regularly smile, or not. We also do gender each and every time we go shopping, starting with the decision on how to shop: online, by mail order, or in a traditional shop.

We do gender again when we check prices, or not, before we buy, when we ask for assistance, or not, and use a shopping list, or not. Ditto when we are willing to walk to the shops, rather than drive, and when, in a supermarket, we systematically work the aisles and wait for items on the shelves to 'hail' us, rather than keep a list of what we want to buy and walk around the store until we find them, and some of us do gender most emphatically when we declare that we 'never go' shopping' and absolutely 'hate' it.

Socialization does not stop on reaching adulthood, but is a project of lifelong learning; as the last chapter showed gender is done differently in old age to how it was done in our youth, and there is less institutional support for it from the high street, which in a small way leads to it being less apparent. The scope which shopping gives individuals in the richer parts of the world, where more shopping goes on, is the most important reason why shopping is important as culture. The key point about the 'situated action' approach mentioned in the last chapter was that developing any skill is a product of both the person and the setting; and both the high street, as a whole, and the individual shop, are settings in which the skill of 'doing' gender is honed.

Shopping as 'doing' gender

West and Zimmerman's stress on gender as something which is not given but has to be achieved or performed, and not just once, but repeatedly, chimes not only with the 'situated action' approach but also Erving Goffman's (1969) 'dramaturgical' approach. This offered a general framework for analysing behaviour in a wide range of social settings, but, as illustration, Goffman often chose examples drawn from behaviour in shops. So, to illustrate how a team works, a team being a group of people who are responsive to each other and know how to put on a performance, he offers the example of salesmen and women who co-operate with each other to 'pull the wool over the customer's eyes'. The dramaturgical possibilities of shopping go a good way towards making shops suitable places for 'doing' gender, as they meet all the conditions outlined by Goffman as necessary for a successful 'performance'. There is the easily identifiable activity (shopping), the fixed boundary (an entrance), the well-demarcated 'front' region (the shop) where the performance is delivered, and a 'back' stage (the tea room, stock room or home) where it is prepared and planned out of sight, and there is a ready supply of actors (other shoppers and shop staff) who can work in teams, whether they are regular team players or thrown together on the day. The point is that they all know how to put on a performance, or applaud one put on by another team. As semi-public spaces, shops encourage a degree of exhibitionism; however, they also free people to make the passing, unsolicited, compliment, such as 'that looks nice', to a stranger, and the reciprocal 'thank you', neither of which would occur outside on the street, or if they did, would have a different meaning.

Behaviour changes when we enter a shop, as a boundary is crossed, and we 'go on stage'. Once inside a shop, providing that an audience is available to witness and cue the performance, for example, the boredom on the face of the man slumped on a sofa outside a changing room where his wife or girlfriend is trying on clothes, the performance will occur. Other acts of 'doing gender' involve teams, and are 'called forth' by the shopping audience, could be the married couple out to buy a bed and testing it, first, by lying on it, and then discussing who is going to pay, or the man testing the strength of a tool. A mother and daughter, or pair of friends out shopping together are both teams performing the 'girls' day out' routine. The theatricality of larger shops with their often very imposing architecture, their neo–classical frontages, window displays, lifts, escalators and banks of lighting, with their mannequins and chorus line of legs in the air (displaying tights), all call forth the performance of gender, but also of class and age; for example, the 'I am a doddery old man' act, so 'please help me nice young lady', and both parties know the script. Even the counter in a little shop is a mini–stage, there to enhance the drama and ritual taking place over it. As a playwright himself, Alan Bennett (2005) was particularly sensitive to the dramatic possibilities of the County Arcade in Leeds, and describes it as having an 'air of whoopee'. Release is one aspect of shopping and people talk more freely to each other inside shops than outside, especially women to women, for inside the shop there is a sense of freedom to become something or someone else.

However, an exceptional case, the story of 'Agnes', illustrates most poignantly how shops can affirm, or fail to affirm, a performance of gender. The point of Harold Garfinkel's (1967) seminal account of 'Agnes', who was in the process of 'transitioning' from living as a man to living as a woman, is to show the importance of tacit knowledge in everyday life. When Garfinkel met Agnes she had been living as a woman for some time and had undergone reconstructive surgery, and even had a boyfriend. However, because she had not grown up as a girl, she had not learned how to dress as a 'normal' woman would have by the time she was in her late teens or early twenties, a failure which was nearly her undoing. The boyfriend appeared not have noticed anything untoward about Agnes, but his mother, her potential mother-in-law had, and Agnes knew that for her relationship to survive she needed to make good her lack of sartorial expertise. But Agnes could not let on what it was that she did not know, or was trying to learn. She could go to dress shops to try to find the right sort of clothes, but did not know what size she was, what might suit her, what was fashionable, or how to 'put an outfit together', and the assistants were not used to giving the sort of advice which she needed. Agnes wanted and needed more from the shop than just a dress, which is an example of the 'more' that shopping gives us, and which we take for granted, because that is the culture of everyday life. While shopping might not spring to mind as the greatest difficulty faced by transsexuals, learning how to buy clothes appropriate for the gender identity which Agnes was adopting required a great deal of tacit knowledge. The shop failed to help Agnes in the way she needed to be helped, a failure which can be interpreted as an example of culture resisting change and reinforcing the existing gender order. Even today, with the godsend of online shopping and websites giving information useful for transsexuals and cross-dressers, for example, by explaining that 'raglan' and 'dolman' sleeves can disguise broad shoulders, if you do not know what a raglan, dolman, or a Magyar, sleeve is, you will still be lost. The problems faced by a transsexual, or transvestite, seeking clothes which are appropriate, and fit, show how the ordinary high street protects or ensures that a conventional gender order is maintained.

Cueing the performance of gender

After public conveniences, or 'rest rooms', shops are the most openly gendered institutions encountered as part of everyday life, and by signalling their gender through their names, décor, displays and goods, often marked as 'for' men or 'for' women, shops coach and coax us into 'doing' ours. You do not have to be too perceptive to see that a shop with the name 'Claire's', and a window full of pink and glitter, is meant for girls, or that one which is highly functional and a monotone electronic grey is arranged to appeal to men and boys. Gender is also a dimension of store design, as managers recognize, and they therefore accommodate the different levels of effort each sex will typically put into shopping. Thus shoe stores often place the men's department on the ground floor to make the whole process easier for them, while women, seen as more intrepid shoppers, are expected to hack it upstairs, even if they have to haul children and buggies along too. Though, perhaps in response to complaints from women about this, more shoe shops now sell to both sexes on the same floor, but at different ends. Most clothing stores are single sex and, as if we could not work out for ourselves which sex, older stores sometimes spell out that they sell clothes 'for men' or 'for women'. Shops selling sports goods, car accessories, electronics, guns and knives are also pretty easy to identify as 'for men', and those selling knitting wool, hosiery, baby wear, or household linen, as 'for women'. The blood, knives and meat of butchers' shops mark them out as distinctly masculine, which makes finding a woman butchering rather than serving meat very surprising.

By contrast, the newly re-emerging sweet shops that sell sweets only (and not cigarettes, papers and top-shelf magazines too), with their colourful and decorative displays, and association with treats, pleasure, women and bounty, are feminine. There are not many shops which are truly 'androgynous', though the pharmacy or chemist's shop is, perhaps, the closest. Given that there are as many female as male pharmacists, and the cosmetics side of the business is very lucrative, pharmacies might be expected to be seen as 'feminine', but the functional décor, white coats and association with medicine, register them as masculine. Once inside a pharmacy, however, the gendering is more obvious, as much of the stock is gendered. Indeed, it can be quite difficult to find a shampoo, shaving foam, or deodorant, which is not marketed as 'for men' or 'for women', and shelved separately, even if, except for their packaging, the products are virtually indistinguishable. When paper tissues arrived on the market they were just that, paper tissues. Then 'stronger' ones, in bigger boxes, were sold 'for men', and soon afterwards softer, quilted ones in pink boxes, impregnated with lotion, appeared on the shelves and were sold 'for women'.

The performance of gender as it is done inside shops is both scripted and improvised and, rather like a pantomime, the show of mutual exasperation put on in shops, perhaps especially by some older couples when attempting to buy clothes for the man, has run for years. Even though the man may have chosen to go shopping because he needs new clothes, and asked his wife or partner to accompany him so that she could give him advice, he still resents it and, once inside a shop, has to put on the performance which shows that he is there under sufferance, mainly to oblige his partner, and wants to get out as fast as possible. If the man is urged to try on the clothes and 'show' his wife or partner what they look like on him, rather than buy them without trying on, this is likely to lead to resistance or a form of passive aggression because, perhaps, it makes him feel like a child jumping to his mother's command. The act of 'I am hating every minute of this' has to be put on, at the same time his wife, her eyes rolled towards her husband register her exasperation, and fortitude at putting up with him. If, by chance, another couple out shopping pass by, one is likely to throw a knowing glance to the other, as an audience is always needed to complete the performance, each couple becoming a 'team' in Goffman's sense.

Men rarely go shopping with other men, whether for clothes or other goods, but if they do, this display will not be part of it, for it only works in the presence of a woman who, merged with the shop, has to be resisted or escaped from. Shops enhance or amplify the performance of gender because of their theatricality; the young couple kissing on an escalator rising through the glass interior of a large modern department stores, might also kiss on the street, but the clinch would not last as long or be done with such élan, if they could not rely on, first, being seen, and, second, an audience which would safely 'look on'. A woman who has picked up some item, walks to another part of the store them and then, fearing she will be seen as a shoplifter, holds the item aloft to show that she is not trying to conceal or steal it, is also doing gender because men do not do the same act. Men do not expect to be challenged, at least not in a shop, and if they are challenged tend to dismiss it more coolly and hold their own, whereas women, both feel more at risk of being challenged, and less confident of either demonstrating their honesty, or escaping the stereotype of the shoplifter as a menopausal, and thus an 'out of her mind' woman. Behaviour changes when people enter shops, as we see in the next chapter too, but it also changes when they leave them, as this means leaving a place of relative order and safety for the disorder and risk of the street.

Risk, barbers and bargaining

As in life, men and women do not face the same risks in relation to shopping, but risk and safety are dimensions of gender, and are reflected in patterns of shopping. In the history of shopping, the rise of the department store in the nineteenth century has been widely seen by feminist historians as a turning point in the emancipation of the bourgeois woman, as it offered her a safe public, indoor space to occupy, where she could socialize without a man to act as a chaperone (Bowlby, 1985). Forty years ago trains in Britain used to reserve one carriage for 'Ladies Only', and some waiting rooms too. Today there is very little space formally designated for either sex, except for washrooms, but each usually knows which are the no-go areas for them and any space strongly identified with one sex is somewhat off-putting for the other one; so the very safety of the department store, which attracted women, repels many men. The classic account of how gender is mapped spatially and the linking of the inside and private sphere with women and femininity, and the outside and public sphere with men and masculinity, is Pierre Bourdieu's (1979) description of the Kabyle household in Algeria, but it is a pattern repeated across many cultures, and reflected in shopping too. Today, most shopping is 'indoors', and the more open to the elements the type of shopping, the more likely it is be competitive and thus to draw men. Against the long-term trend of shopping becoming progressively feminized, the historical masculinity of shopping survives only in the open-air street market with its 'barrow boys' and showmanship; and though both sexes work on market stalls today, there are fewer women doing so than men, and the women cannot do the traditional 'patter' of the market vendor, which is largely to tease and chat up women. The twentieth-century version of the pedlar, the 'door-to-door' salesman', had a reputation of being dangerous to housebound women, who were seen as easy prey. Though as a species they are now almost extinct, certainly in countries such as Britain and the United States, where travelling salesmen still exist, as in Mexico, this sleazy reputation has followed, with rural women seen as their victims as the salesmen travel around, offering often highly sexualized fantasies of escape, hand in hand with loan sharks to make those fantasies seem possible.

The element of outside as representing danger and masculinity is kept alive in the high street by the barber shop, which is still called 'a shop', though not always thought of as one, in contrast to the more interior term 'salon', favoured by hairdressers with a female clientele. Cutting men's hair was a trade traditionally pursued in the open air, and in some places still is. If the barber shop is not 'on the street', it is 'open to the street', and scissors and razors, and the risk they represent are a spectacle for passersby. Some barbers, even in rich modern societies, keep the traditional open-fronted format and lines of men squashed together on a bench waiting their turn as a retro feature. While today it may be more common for both sexes to use the same 'hairdresser', the traffic is one way, as men enter the women's domain, the hairdresser, more easily than women do the barber shop, a general pattern of women's 'spaces' being found more hospitable, or permeable, than those of men.

Risk is always relative, but whatever the order of risk, it serves as a mark of gender in shopping as in other areas of life, as shopping by bargaining illustrates. Where bargaining remains an everyday practice, done by men, women and children, everyone does it with ease, and bargaining is not a mark of gender. But where bargaining is not normal practice, it appears to be something men find comes quite easily when they try, because it is more congruent with current ideas about masculinity. This was illustrated by one of Harold Garfinkel's (1969) 'breaching experiments', designed to expose the implicit, and often very fragile, understandings upon which everyday life is based. An experiment which could not be done today for ethical reasons, it was done by Garfinkel who asked his students to enter a shop where bargaining would not be expected, for example, a pharmacy, and then to bargain for some low-priced item. Garfinkel then split this group of students into two and asked half to bargain just once, and the other half to bargain repeatedly. Then, splitting that group too, half were told to bargain for both expensive and inexpensive goods. Most of the students got used to bargaining, and those who did more of it got more skilled and, indeed, some were so impressed with their success that they planned to repeat the exercise in their own time. However, some of the students could not bargain at all, and though Garfinkel does not give the sexes of the students my guess is that if they included women then these were the drop-outs. Bearing this study in mind when teaching about gender I have sometimes asked students, mainly women, how they felt about bargaining, and more than once was told a story of how a boyfriend, after agreeing to accompany the student, his girlfriend, to buy clothes would, just as she was about to pay, and to her acute embarrassment, ask the assistant for a discount for cash.

Timing was clearly important, and to my astonishment my son did the same when, accompanying me to a buy a television set in a Sony store, not a place where I, at least, thought bargaining was a common practice, he used exactly the same tactic. He had engaged the salesman in a technical discussion, though it was clear that the television was for me and that I was paying, then, at the point of payment, my son asked for, and got, a student discount. The chance to bargain, which I did not spot, was a challenge and one, perhaps, which appeals more to most men than to most women. Maybe there are many more settings where bargaining would work, but women do not see them.

Though both sexes can, and do, enjoy a bargain, how they arrive at one is different; the sharp eyes of the woman may spot a bargain, because she keeps a close eye on stock in shops, but she is unlikely to feel very comfortable bargaining. Traders know this, and often do not offer, or expect, women to bargain with them. This is why it is not uncommon for car salesmen to think that selling a car to a woman is a piece of cake because they just accept the asking price, whereas men always bargain for a deal. The point is that where bargaining is not normal practice, it still seems to come quite easily to men when they attempt it. This is because bargaining fits with a broad sense of masculinity, heterosexual and homosexual, but not with the more compliant and less competitive code of behaviour which, in the West, is femininity. There are parts of the world, for example, West Africa, where women traders bargain very assertively and this does not, in any way, undermine their femininity. Whereas, in Western culture, despite an ideology of gender equality, women being decidedly assertive, in relation to bargaining, or any other activity, remains tricky. So tricky, in fact, that one study on household work, using US and Australian data, found that American wives earning more than their husbands absolutely could not, as bargaining theory would predict they should, succeed in getting those husbands to do more housework; and moreover, they ended up raising their hours of domestic labour to 'compensate' for their husband's 'gender deviance', as the authors' put it 'gender trumps money (see Bittman *et al.*, 2003). Bargaining is not just an individual skill, or an aspect of gender, it is also 'situated action', thus a person who would not dream of bargaining in a department store, may find it quite easy at a car boot or porch sale, or, when abroad, if instructed by the guide book that this is 'what you do'.

The auction

There are more or less masculine, or more or less feminine, ways of shopping and, at a pinch, whatever our sex, we can adopt the style of the other one, if cued and supported by the setting. The risk, competition and 'exteriority' which, in some combination, are part of bargaining, barter and barbering, are also part of masculinity and are present in the auction, which is another way of buying if not one we often think of as shopping (except, perhaps, for eBay). Like the traditional market, the auction is a public test of character, of skill, focus and stamina, and it attracts men more than women. Some of the goods auctioned are not normally sold in shops, but cars, pictures, and antiques are, which make the auction an alternative mode. Once, after I was overheard saying that I was 'working on shopping', the man sitting beside me took this as a cue to launch into a speech about how much he disliked that activity, how he never entered a shop without always knowing exactly what he wanted to buy, even a toolshop, and always bought only what he needed, never what he wanted, and how he was never waylaid, distracted or seduced into buying on impulse. Then his wife, overhearing these words, whispered 'Auction?' At which point he sweetly smiled and admitted that he found auctions a very agreeable way of spending time, often got carried away at them, and could speedily convert a want into a need and come home with something which he had not planned to buy.

The auction did not count as shopping for this man, though his behaviour turned out to match his description of what shopping meant to him, and which was something which he claimed never to do. Implicitly, to have acted in that way would be to behave as a woman shopper does, and this would undermine his masculinity, so it was not how he behaved. Though exactly the same behaviour at the auction strengthened, rather than diminished, his self image as a man. The auction was shopping as adventure, and a test of character. Though it has an element of secrecy, the auction is anything but intimate, and has nothing to do with home, clothes, or getting undressed in a semi-public place. A highly controlled, collective haggling situation, where a price is fixed by the whole group through desire, indifference and competition, the auction is, for many men, the antithesis of the claustrophobic, cosy, cloying and feminine atmosphere of the shop. A very male affair, and a very public form of buying, as other people know both what a buyer has bought, and how much they paid for it, however much or little that might be, the auction makes every buyer a winner. Buying on the online auction site eBay has some of the same qualities too. Though done at home, a more cosy place, and not quite so public, it involves competition and risk, calculating when to bid, following the bidding as tension builds, and a last few seconds every bit as heart-stopping as any football final. Cross cultural anthropologist Geert Hofstede (1998), highlighting Britain as a particular example, sees masculinity and femininity as the two poles of a single dimension and suggests that deep gender divisions are due to particularly deep social divisions overall and a particularly masculine national culture. A more technological explanation might be the extremely high take up of internet connection in Britain, and other comparable countries, as this makes it very easy for men to continue to 'do' gender by disavowing shopping, or by claiming that they never go shopping, because shopping online does not involve physically entering a shop.

Ambivalence, subtlety and disavowal

A major problem when discussing gender is our often ambivalent relationship towards generalization, in the form of the gender stereotype, as this is something most of us both endorse and resist. The moment we claim that younger men are not as afraid of, or bored by, the idea of shopping as older men, we remember someone we know who is. There are, of course, always exceptions, and if generalizations about gender are particularly tricky it may be because, as Hofstede points out, this difficulty of discussing gender is a form of taboo and, as with all taboos, it protects some 'sacred' value from being revised, which it might be if more discussion took place. The cultural pressure on men, of all ages, to 'do' gender remains as great as it ever was, and if one way in which gender, in societies with especially masculine cultures, is by disavowing shopping, it will continue to be done in this way if, perhaps, more subtly. Quite a young man, thoughtful enough to discuss the matter with me, told of how he would never say that he was 'going shopping', but was comfortable telling his girlfriend that he would 'go to' or 'call in at' the shops on the way home. 'Going to the shops' did not seem as aimless as 'going shopping', whereas 'calling in' made it clear that shopping was a secondary activity. Hard-working and ambitious, it was important for this young man to be, and to be seen as, purposive. 'Just looking' was an anathema to him, as it may be for many men, because shopping trips often seem not to produce a tangible result. The association of shopping with buying clothes, and taking time over it, led this young man to see the activity as feminine and therefore to claim not to do it. However, prompted by his girlfriend, he was reminded that on a visit to California the year before he had bought masses of clothes, which he explained as a 'once a year blow-out', and saw as acceptable because it was efficient. Women, too, have blow-outs, but are more likely to describe them as 'binges', which is not a word the man would have used of himself because of its association with weakness, drunkenness, bulimia and being a woman.

The dislike of shopping often expressed by many men is generally less a dislike of shopping per se, than of shopping in the way women shop, or the way men think women shop, which is not as they do, or think they do, namely, fast and effectively. Of course, not all men see themselves in this way, and even those who do are often rather selective in their professed concern with time, and will often happily spend hours online researching items to buy, or settle down for an evening to look at a catalogue of gadgets. Of English men in particular, social anthropologist Kate Fox (2004) observes that there is almost an unwritten rule among them which prohibits any enjoyment of shopping or, at least, of showing any such enjoyment, as that might be seen as effeminate. The correct masculine line, Fox notes, is to 'define any shopping one does, including the purchase of luxuries and inessentials, as something that has to be done, a means to an end, never a pleasure in itself'. It is a view supported by the survey 'Men Uncovered' (2004) commissioned by *The Observer* newspaper which found that twenty per cent of British men actively hated shopping, and would try to avoid it if they could, and another forty per cent did 'not particularly enjoy it', whereas only four per cent of women claimed to hate shopping, and eighteen per cent to 'not particularly enjoy it. The key point is that for shopping to be agreeable, at least for British men, it has to fit their image of masculinity.

Shopping and masculinity: heterosexual or homosexual?

Disavowing shopping, claiming to either hate or love it, and seizing every opportunity to 'rubbish' the way the other sex approaches the task, is 'doing masculinity', or rather, heterosexual masculinity, as this largely means showing that you are not like a woman. If shopping is feminine, then 'the shop' too, as a symbol of the female body, in the wrong place, can be very off-putting for men or, at least, for heterosexual men. Keeping a distance, at least in public, from women and all things associated with them, is largely what drives men to disavow shopping, but it is only half the problem. For 'being good at shopping' is stereotypically what gay men are good at, so, consciously, or not, this stereotype drives straight men to distance themselves further from the activity. Being seen as 'good at shopping', for gay men, however, does not undermine their sense of masculinity, though being crap at it might. When purchasing is made more masculine by being more challenging, competitive and game-like, it is not resisted so fervently, which is why bargaining and auctions appeal more to men than to women, and why men are better at them. Quite possibly this is because bargaining is an extension of the negotiating techniques into which boys are inducted by the 'swap' culture as children and young teenagers, at the same age as girls are getting into shopping. However, it was not ever thus, and where shopping is seen as men's work it is openly enjoyed by them too; and ditto, taking an interest in clothes, at least by those with the means to buy more than one set a time. Historically the 'dandy' was a male figure, who far outshone his female companion in colour, detail, decoration and expense.

However, where professing to dislike shopping and, particularly to dislike shopping for clothes is normative for men, it is done with vigour and assertiveness. Still, much of what men profess is irritating for them about the process of shopping, as opposed to the very idea, the queues and the crowds, the things to carry, and walkways not designed to get you from A to B as quickly as possible, but force you to pass by yet more goods, also irritate women. But women do not so regularly complain about shopping, partly because it is not a challenge to their gender identity in the same way as for men, for whom being fast and good at 'finishing the job' is a part of their masculinity, and partly because they have adapted to accept what they largely cannot avoid, which includes shopping. If it is sometimes said of women that they think about shopping as often as men think about sex, it must be remembered that eighty per cent of all evening meals are still cooked by women in Britain (Nicolaas, 1995) and that whoever cooks usually finds it most efficient to buy the ingredients also. Then, if they are buying food, they usually also buy other household goods too, so a shopping list is at the back of the mind of whoever does most cooking and provisioning for most of the day, whatever their sex.

Chapter 2 gave an account of shopping's 'fall from grace' as the industrial revolution destroyed household-based production and, as a consequence, housekeeping and women's reputations as careful consumers. The chance to show prudence seemed lost to women as they became stigmatized as spendthrifts and, even if a slight exaggeration, women cannot today be seen as prudent because this virtue has migrated to men who, stereotypically, see themselves as 'efficient' shoppers in contrast to women who, in the men's view, are not. Some men see their shopping as 'collecting' and, because they do not count buying online or picking up some cigarettes, as shopping, they narrow the meaning of shopping to 'women shopping' or to 'shopping for clothes'. One further consequence, perhaps especially for the older generation, is that many men take it for granted that someone else will buy most of their food and clothes for them, which in some households is exactly what happens. Indeed some older women have been buying their husband's clothes for so long that those husbands no longer know their own size, let alone their wife's size. To some degree the purchasing of clothes for men by women is done as a solution to the problem women often face of finding a suitable present for their husbands, sons or brothers, which is sometimes a win–win situation as the men get the clothes and avoid shopping and the women solve the present problem. Often, too, money is saved, for women return the clothes if they are not right, though if they buy them in the first place, they are more likely to be 'right'. This is not a female supremacist point but, if going to shops is disliked by men, returning goods to them is disliked even more, and less frequently done.

Married men, though they generally do less shopping than their wives, also have to find a different way of doing it, and one solution is to play a part in buying larger goods, especially those which involve technology, as this gives the men a chance to offer technical expertise as a form of caring, even though many of the machines which men feel most qualified to choose, washing machines or vacuum cleaners (especially Dysons), are not those which they use themselves. However, these goods still get 'looked over' by the men, and men still often make the final decision, even if the preliminary 'scoping' is done by women. The failure to recognize that the person who uses, and the person who determines what is bought, are not necessarily the same, was a lesson learned in the 1930s when a range of new electrical domestic appliances, such as carpet cleaners, failed to take off, despite having been heavily marketed as labour-saving devices *for* women, because the decision about purchasing such large items did not rest with women, but with their husbands, who did not use the appliances (Bowden and

Offner, 1996). It was not until the marketers took note of this and aimed their marketing at men that sales of the machines picked up. Men may not do as much shopping as women, but this does not mean that they do not powerfully influence what is bought. Who chooses what to buy is far more complex than who pays at the till. This is a point, too, made by Mary Douglas (1997) when explaining how while women might go to the shops more than men, once there, the choices which the women make have already been made for them by the 'cultural bias' of their homes and their marriages.

Two different gender cultures

Second-wave feminism may have increased a mutual resolve for both sexes to overcome traditional patterns and share domestic tasks more equally. However, problems still arise because, even with the best will in the world, gender still affects how we think things should be done. This is illustrated by one couple who tried to rationalize their shopping by establishing a central list on the computer. Keen shoppers, equally committed to sharing all domestic tasks, and equally proud of being well organized, their decision to set up the central list on the computer was a joint one. However, a problem arose over whether to arrange the list, by goods, or by aisle. The couple eventually agreed on the aisle option, but it soon broke down because each liked to shop in different supermarkets and, without a uniform aisle system across stores, their system did not work. Unused to failure, but faced with the prospect of having to jettison either their commitment to sharing all tasks, or their pride in being well organized, they began to fear that they were not as compatible as they had imagined themselves to be.

Disentangling the effects of gender from marriage, or cohabitation, can be difficult, but is important; and as Gillian Dunne (1998) has shown, when 'gender is held constant', as it is in same-sex partnerships, the basis on which domestic work is shared is quite different from that of heterosexual partnerships, or mixed-sex households. In student households, often mixed sex, and not necessarily based on couples, female students typically find it difficult to get their male flatmates to shop or clean for the whole household, and not just for themselves, if even that.

Still, many people, women especially, idealize shared activities, including 'shopping together', whether on a regular basis or as a special occasion. Even so, couples may start out together, then go their separate ways, and meet up later at a set time or point, because they know that if they stay together, issues of collaboration will arise over who holds the list, or the trolley, and who has to run around seeking out odd items. The difficulty of co-operation is not individual wilfulness, or selfishness, but culture, and the less you do of any activity, whether that is shopping or fixing the car, the less good at doing it you become, and the less willing to express a view on it, other than that you have none. One powerful reason why many heterosexual men dislike shopping with their partners is that they dislike feeling 'put on the spot' when asked for an opinion about some product in which they have absolutely no interest. Another example of Mary Douglas's(1997) point about shopping bringing out differences or, in her words, being 'agonistic', is as it is used by individuals to 'distance' themselves from those with whom they do not see themselves as belonging, and will make more effort to ensure that they are not seen in that way by others. Finding out which group we belong to is, including those defined by sexuality, becomes more of a preoccupation in adolescence, and some places for doing this are more congenial than others.

A midway place

The last chapter touched on how both sexes indulge in a bit of experimental shoplifting in the teenage years and how, for urban teenagers, shops and shopping centres are where the kids 'let off steam', but did not explore in any detail how shopping fosters the complicated and erratic process of developing and affirming a gender identity. Adolescence, midway between childhood and adulthood, is a critical moment in establishing a gender identity, and the midway position of shops and shopping districts, between home and school, is part of what leads shops and shopping centres to be bent to this task. It is perhaps easiest to see how this might operate in the way children, at least those living in towns, and who are not bussed to and from school, stage their journeys home from school by calling in at shops where they feel themselves to be beyond the reach of parents or teachers. The time spent in shops by schoolchildren after school, is a form of 'wind down' time similar to that of a man having a drink in the pub on the way home, but it is not solitary as that tends to be, and is done in a group, a single-sex group which reverses what, up to that point, is a trend for children's friendship groups to become more mixed. At younger ages, most friendship groups are single sex, but these tend to dissolve as adolescence approaches and sexuality comes into play, but not around shops where, perhaps to get away from the particular pressures of the mixed-sex classroom, latency age schoolchildren and young adolescents reform into single-sex groups and head off for single-sex settings, such as the shops. This pattern perhaps bears comparison to the way progression to adulthood, particularly for boys, is organized in many traditional and rural African societies, where a period of withdrawal to a different and isolated place is required for them to become recognized as men.

In his study of the rites of passage among the Ndembu, Victor Turner (1970) argued that it was not only the withdrawal and isolation which was critical, but the place to which the young men went had also to be 'liminal', that is, indeterminate, ambiguous, timeless and disorienting, as these were the qualities which effected the change from boy to man. Most of the shops frequented by groups of schoolchildren living in highly urbanized Western societies are not isolated, ambiguous or indeterminate, but they often are timeless and disorienting, and many have a sense of creative ambiguity and possibility about them that is both what attracts, and makes them places for trying on, or rehearsing, new identities. The use made of shops and shopping centres by teenagers, for sorting out stuff other than goods on sale, is wholly informal, but that teenagers do use such places for such purposes lay behind the decision in Britain to ban, or attempt to ban from shopping centres individuals in groups of four or more who were wearing 'hoodies'. Though it seems, ludicrous, a crowd of teeming children can quite often appear dangerous to the shopkeeper, and also to older customers, who fear being pushed and shoved; however, ambiguously, the sense of risk and possibility which might frighten the older age group, can attract the younger one. The role of shops and shopping spaces as civic or public spaces is considerable and, as Sharon Zukin (2004) observes, writing about North America, shops are among the few places left in 'the over-controlled and fear-ridden urban environment, where 'creativity and control can be balanced'. However, while for a period teenage boys may find shopping centres a draw, it is an interest which they more often grow through than retain, in contrast to girls of the same age. This relates to a point made by Lyn Mikel Brown and Carol Gilligan (1992) about early adolescence being a period of 'psychological footbinding' for girls, and a moment of change when the girls begin to lose their 'voice', their confidence, sassiness and courage, and take on the traditional stereotype of women as submissive, non-combative and self effacing. Though Brown and Gilligan are discussing girls of a generation ago, their point may still hold; and if it corresponds in any way to what the shops which the girls frequent in this period of their lives mean to them, it is very complex. For the uses made of shops and shopping reinforce the pull of the traditional gender identity, but also serve as a haven from it, as most boys of the same age who, by this time will have 'dis-identified' with their mothers, and certainly from going shopping with them, will also have learned to give shops and shopping a wide berth.

6

Putting on a Posh Voice

Is closing the village shop a tragedy? Does another Tesco spell the end of community? Did food rationing 'keep the peace' in Britain during the two world wars, or Wal-Mart save New Orleans? The cross talk about shopping is confusing. For criminologist Ian Taylor (1999) the private and self-policing shopping mall was the 'central iconic building' of the 'new urban imaginary' and, with its 'self-contained corporate office buildings, fast food and leisure facilities and private car parking lots', sent a message to the poor that they had no place in it. Yet the mall is a great deal easier for those in a wheelchair or using a walking aid to move around in than the narrow, uneven and often crowded pavement, and thus helps more people to live an 'ordinary life'. Managing to 'still shop for myself' is much cherished as a mark of independence by the old and disabled, while for those cursed by being so well known that they cannot nip out to the shops without being mobbed or photographed, the ordinariness of so doing is a priceless, and lost, privilege. For new arrivals in a foreign city, stumbling on a shop selling familiar products labelled in their own tongue can be a lifeline, but not for those unable to read those languages or recognize most of the goods, who may find the same shop unnerving, intrusive and inhospitable. For a working-class woman fearing that she will be seen as a shop lifter, shopping can sharpen the experience of class; but for one using shops as an 'open college' it may flatten it. The charity shop, with prices low enough to allow all customers to feel that, if they want, they can afford to buy anything in the shop, puts everyone on an equal footing, and comes near to giving everyone an experience normally enjoyed only by the very rich. There is no solution to the paradox that shopping both includes and excludes, because these are two sides of the same coin.

This chapter takes as given the dual nature of shopping and explores its effects. The first two sections start with how class is inscribed in shopping, initially in a very categorical way, and then more subtly or insidiously, through the opportunities offered by the large, well-lit supermarket or department store, and by the spread of self service, to 'do' class by looking at and looking down on other people. Then, turning the picture around altogether, the latter two sections of the chapter look at how shops, which are private institutions, can and do help to deliver a range of 'public goods' or services, including some of the equality which is promised by citizenship, and in ways which do help 'hold us together'.

From 'The Stores' to the 'John Lewis list'

Class is an embedded part of shopping, in the first place because where we live is usually also where we do most of our shopping; and, while some residential districts are socially mixed, many more are not. Where districts and shops are mixed, there is no let up as shops are badged by class through their names, addresses, frontages, stock, and by their type. The pie shop, betting shop, fish and chip shop, 'pound' shop and charity shop, have working-class associations, while the book shop, outdoor pursuits or sheet-music shop have middle-class ones. In Britain a select few shops bear the Royal Crest over their entrances, which shows that at some time they sold some goods to some member of the Royal Family, who was then so pleased that they awarded the right to display this 'crest' to that shop, which then suggests to any casual passerby that they might think twice before entering, in case they just might not 'fit in'. However it is not only shops themselves which are badged in this way; different forms of shopping have class associations too. So the street market or the 'Ann Summers' 'party' are seen as working class, while the department store is seen as a more middle-class institution. The chain store, placed somewhere in between, is seen as lower middle class; and its customers may be more mixed; in Britain, at least, they will know whether or not they are 'slumming it' or getting 'a bit above themselves'. Except in the case of self service, class is embedded in the language of shopping too, because shopping is the context in which individuals are most likely to be addressed as 'Sir' or 'Madam', and the relationship between the customer and the shopworker re-enacts that of personal service. Though not always respectfully. For example one friend was greeted as she entered an upmarket kitchen shop, but soaked from a sudden downpour, with, 'Madam, I don't think we have anything here for you.' The manner in which class is reproduced, or reinforced, through shopping is not always as brutal as this but it has been as clear cut.

The 'Army and Navy Store' in Victoria Street London, or just 'The Stores', as it was known, was initially established to supply goods and guns as well as food and clothing to fighting men and their families; but not to all fighting men, only officers or their widows who had to be members and pay an annual subscription fee. 'Other ranks' were left to fend for themselves in some other way until three years after the First World War when the Navy Army Air Force Institute (NAAFI) was established as 'the official trading organization of HM Forces', and pointedly announced that it was to provide 'retail and leisure services to the services' for all ranks. Even so, the class attachment to 'The Stores' and its catalogue remained intact and was much depended on by overseas civil servants, officers and white 'settlers' to help them keep up something of the lifestyle which they felt they had left behind when taking up the 'burden' of running the colonies. The writer Doris Lessing (1994), brought up by parents who had hoped to find a better life through farming in Rhodesia, remembers how the Army and Navy catalogue 'regulated our lives as it did those of middle-class children anywhere in the colonies'.

The formalized link between class and access to the 'Stores' was unusual, but even without the paraphernalia of membership and subscription fees, shops still serve as class landmarks as much as they do geographical ones. Writing about the County Arcade in Leeds, the city where he grew up, Alan Bennett (2005) describes how each shop in the Arcade had an intense personal and social significance, such that walking through it was an exercise in knowing your place, especially when passing the shop 'where we got our school blazers, but didn't get those great class indicators, the Cash's name tapes that better-class boys had sewn into all their clothes'. A microcosm of the wider society, Bennett sees the Arcade, as a whole, marking 'the border of respectability', and describes how beyond it was where the 'less orthodox retail establishments' lay, the herbalists and the 'shops selling surgical appliances, rubber goods, remedies for haemorrhoids or hair, wanted and unwanted, and remedies for babies too, wanted and unwanted'. The sense of a social order which has to be physically represented in the department store keeps menswear and womenswear apart, if possible on different floors, with menswear generally on a higher floor than womenswear, and traditionally places more expensive goods, such as antiques and oriental carpets, higher still. The same sense of social order led to the basement being the place for the bargains, 'ends' and 'rejects', just like the people who bought them. Though that practice is dying out, save for a few discount stores such as 'Filene's' in the United States, it survives through the convention that the basement, or 'downstairs', which in the home is where the servants belong, continues to be where goods connected with domestic labour, cooking, cleaning and DIY, are placed, whereas living room furniture, which represents leisure, is placed on a higher floor.

Times, of course, change, and so does class. Keeping up with the change are a clutch of stores in Britain which Stephen Pollard and Andrew Adonis (1997) describe as 'suppliers by appointment to the classless middle class', and single out, in particular, Marks and Spencer, Laura Ashley and John Lewis. The last mentioned store was used, through the 'John Lewis list', as a bench mark to guide Members of Parliament about what they could expect the state to pay for furnishing their second homes before the 2009 scandal of parliamentary expenses put an end to the system, a precision matching of store to class, or rather, a class fraction, the British political class. The list of factors, social, demographic, economic, political, technical, national and global, which have contributed to change in class relations in Western industrialized nations are far too complex to do more than list as above. But the net result in most of the richer nations has been a decline of manual occupations, a rise of service and IT related ones, of more women working, more higher education, more migration, and less organized labour. A change in the overall shape of the social structure, marked by a distinct growth of the middle class and a contraction of the working class, was the first and most striking feature to be noted, and explored by commentators. Attention then shifted more to whether the basis of class had changed with newer patterns of ownership, particularly home ownership (Saunders, 1982, 1990), and whether lifestyle had become more salient than occupation, and then to whether, with changing class ratios, class relations were altering too.

Sociologist Frank Parkin (1979) argued that they were, and one feature which he singled out was that at the interpersonal level, relations between middle and working-class people were no longer as strongly marked by condescension and deference, as once they had been. Class difference had not disappeared, nor class relations, but they had, as Parkin saw it, taken an 'individualistic turn' and been replaced by two competing class strategies. These were the 'exclusionary' strategies of the privileged class, intent on remaining privileged, and the 'usurpatory' strategies of aspiring classes, who aimed to join or replace the existing elite. Snobbery is the classic example of an 'exclusionary' strategy, though increasingly strategies which involve 'changing the goal posts' are used, for example, the move towards making design and taste 'difficult' to understand so that it is not easily adopted or imitated. The classic example of the 'usurpatory' strategy is 'marrying' or 'buying in' to the elite or, if these fail, of pressing for more reward by merit. Both sorts of strategy are pursued individualistically, not collectively, not least because we can only marry one at a time. Parkin also identified what he called the 'boundary problem', by which he meant an increasing difficulty in accurately identifying a person's class, especially a young person's, by their accent, address, clothing, or even occupation. For the middle classes, who had traditionally felt quite free to act in a condescending way towards working-class people, the risk of the personal consequences which would follow if they offended someone they would rather not, were just too great. So they had, in Parkin's view, cleaned up their act, and improved their manners towards working-class people in general, at least in the way which they spoke to them. It was different in the past and one friend, from a working-class background, remembers how he and his siblings used to laugh at their mother for putting on what he called 'a posh voice' when she went into a shop, perhaps because she felt that she would be treated rather better? This may not quite count as a 'usurpatory strategy', but it would be more surprising today.

Accompanying this shift towards a less openly class-based pattern of interaction has been 'retailization' and the 'service revolution' which, together, have led customers from all classes to take for granted an improvement in the manners of shop staff. But there is a twist. All customers have not been through the same training as shop staff, and do not all feel equally obliged to be equally respectful of all other customers. As a result, not everyone feels equally at ease inside shops because of how social class is still 'done' by the middle class towards the working class, not verbally, but by looking. This may be the moment to cite social historian E. P. Thompson's (1963) famous statement that 'class is not a thing but a relationship' and that 'if history could be stopped at a given point there would be no classes to see, only a multitude of individuals with a multitude of experiences'. It is because of some of those experiences, which include being patronized, 'get under our skin' and turn into a relationship with ourselves, that class is perpetuated. The social historian most obviously following in Thompson's footsteps as a historian of class in the British Isles has been David Cannadine (1998) who describes an 'all- pervasive consciousness of class' in Britain as the most distinctive feature of British life, and which has Britons 'always thinking about who they are, what kind of society they belong to, and where they themselves belong in it'.

Shopping through the looking class

The constant preoccupation with placing oneself and others within a class structure is done in all sorts of contexts, including when shopping. Thus one woman, writing for Mass Observation, states 'Never has the phrase "You are what you eat" been more obvious than when looking in other people's supermarket baskets! Large people seem to have baskets filled with lots of bread and cakes and ready meals and special offers. Slim people seem to have baskets of vegetarian meals, and buy flowers and candles and specialist bread. Large families seem to have large dogs, who are bought huge tins of dog food, but all in one flavour.' Nonetheless, she also adds gratefully that looking in other people's baskets sometimes reminded her of things which she needed, but had 'forgotten to get, despite a good list'.

Some shoppers, if careful not to 'look down' on working–class people, still cannot stop themselves from being critical of their 'lifestyle', or what they think of as the working-class lifestyle. The same woman cited above was 'aware of people not really liking others to see exactly what is in their shopping trolley'. She was right. A British Caribbean man, talking specifically about shopping at Marks and Spencer, said that he felt that he was always being followed around by 'these high and mighty people who look down upon you' with 'a wee glance of basket snobbery' to register the basket's contents, and then show surprise if they include healthy Quorn–like food, which he imagines leads them to think, 'What's he doing buying such things?' For the people being 'looked at' and 'looked down upon' in this way, it is as de–personalizing as it is for any woman being stared at as a sex object. They know they are being looked as an example of the whole class, not as an individual, and they feel diminished. In this respect, contesting Parkin's claim that class relations had taken an individualistic turn, and that all working-class people or people of colour were all the same, the issue is who looks and who is looked at, and what they feel about it. For a middle-class person, being looked at may feel uncomfort-able, but they are more likely to view the other person as rude than to feel themselves as diminished. For the working-class person being looked at in shops, or anywhere else, leads to the classic 'hidden injury', an interior sense of unease.

Cannadine makes the point that 'class consciousness', which leads to political action, is not the same as 'consciousness of class', which has more the opposite effect and produces a paralysing self consciousness which normalizes inequality, and thereby helps maintain the status quo. In Cannadine's words, 'class is what culture does to inequality'. To illustrate this, let's consider some of the responses when the Mass Observation Archive asked its panel of writers to describe their experiences of using shopping to 'make a difference' (Mass Observation 'Shopping as Making a Difference' Summer Directive 2007). A broad theme, this request was clearly open to wide interpretation. However the Archive, as is its practice, gave various examples of the sorts of difference which it had had mind when choosing this topic, for example, whether and how much it meant to the writers to boycott goods from certain countries for political reasons, or, say, to support animal welfare, Fair Trade or environmental issues, or simply to be patriotic. While it is also a rule of the Archive to ask contributors to write only from personal experience, not to write about other people or to use names or any other personal identifier, in other respects the writers are free to interpret the topics in any way they like. The writers know these rules and while observations about others (though not names) are often slipped in, in this case while the contributors wrote about the sorts of issues mentioned by the 'directive', many also seized the opportunity to write about looking in 'other people's shopping baskets'. This was a practice widely confessed to by both sexes and was much enjoyed, even if it also made some feel a little guilty.

One woman wrote, 'I am still amazed by how many people seem to have tinned fruit and vegetables in their trolleys -- it makes no sense to me'; she also wrote of how she liked guessing who the people were buying for, and that she was always intrigued to know whether 'the trolley of white sliced bread and margarine (was) for an institution, or a one-off tea party. . . ?' Another woman wrote, a little more self consciously, of noticing 'a woman with children who had bumper bags of crisps and sweets, and supermarket brand frozen pizzas, and massive bottles of soft drink in her trolley', and how this had led her, the writer, to think 'How can you be feeding your kids that muck?' This woman also describes seeing 'an overweight woman with two quite plump kids buying lots of fatty foods and sugary stuff', which leads to certain thoughts, but then she checks herself and reflects that 'this was a bit judgemental, I hate myself when I am like this, because it is only one day in someone's life – perhaps they buy healthy, non-processed foods the rest of the time and this day is an exception'. Another woman, on seeing someone else buying an iron in Tesco's, found herself wanting to ask that woman whether it was an 'an impulse buy, or whether hers was broken, and then whether she had actually come to Tesco's to buy one?', for, as the writer explains, it would never have occurred to her to shop for an iron in Tesco's.

This constant observing of social difference cannot be helped; it is part of Western culture and is little different from a farmer, fisherman or pilot always having an eye to the weather. The urge to compare and contrast, and take oneself as the standard by which to judge other people, is encouraged by the abundance of goods in modern shops and, in particular, by self service which make shopping an activity requiring constant comparison and speedy rejection or acceptance. Self service can be very self serving, and is a different experience from shopping where you are offered goods by a shopkeeper or assistant, in the course of which you discuss the merits of different products with them, and might as a result change your mind. This older form of shopping continues in some shops, such as jewellers, car showrooms and when buying wedding dresses, but it is not the most common form of shopping any longer. Many of the Mass Observation writers admitted to how 'looking in other people's baskets' gave them 'a pleasurable feeling of superiority', and several confessed to how they liked, as one writer put it, 'see whether anyone has as many sorts of fruit and vegetables as I do and (I) feel smug and self satisfied if they don't'. Conversely, one of the most painful of 'hidden injuries' is the result of looking poor, of feeling that you are 'found wanting', and then feeling that you are 'never allowed to forget it' and have your appearance 'held against you'. As one woman, talking about shopping at Marks and Spencer, explained 'You could dress up smart, go in there and buy an item, anything, a pair of socks, right? And they'd say "Thank you, madam" and put it in a bag. Or you could go home, get your kids, throw your hair up in a pony tail, put your leggings on, your trainers and an old mac, and they'd say "Thank you". Where's the Madam gone?'

If class can often only be seen through its effects, the effects often happen through being seen, and through how we respond to being seen. As one young mum described it, one effect of looking 'normally harassed, with trousers and leggings' was, she said, enough 'to have them watching you' so that 'you can feel their eyes on your back as you are walking around'. To dispel this impression she felt obliged to put on a performance of 'keeping something at a level where they can see it. I'm always doing this. I shouldn't feel it . . ., but I'm going, I've got this and I'm going to the checkout (and you've got it at their eye level, haven't you). So I'm going to go over here first but I've still got it and I haven't put it anywhere.' This is 'doing' class, as a performance which says, 'Yes, I am working class, but I am not a thief.' On hearing this account, another woman added that if her kids started to pester her inside a shop, and she looked 'a bit manic', 'they', meaning the managers, would 'go for you', even though 'there's probably someone over there stealing their safe (but) they're following *you* around'. Imagining how you are seen is a crucial part of 'internalization' and for the working-class women with whom we talked, it was essentially persecutory. If someone else sees you as 'bad' it is not long before you begin to believe it too. You may be livid, but it is hard to be indifferent.

Looks, looking at, and being looked at, are all part of relationships, and can be felt as loving and affirming, or as a preliminary to an attack. Young men, the social group most likely to be mugged, soon learn how not to make eye contact so that they may avoid the challenge, 'What are you looking at, then?' The capacity to imagine what another person might be thinking or feeling from their facial expressions has many implications and is central to the 'theory of the mind', widely seen as having been critical to the evolutionary 'success' of humankind. In the shorter time frame of one human life, how we come to know ourselves is the result both of how others see us, and how we think they see us. The quality of the relationship which an infant has with its mother can turn on how she looks *to* that infant and how she looks *at* it, with a smiling face, a 'dead' unresponsive one or a frightening stare (see Winnicott, 1967;

Wright, 1991). Because of the long period of neonatal dependency, human beings have evolved to become very sensitive to visual expression and the experience of relationships because their lives depend on it; an infant cannot survive unless someone cares for it, and to keep caring the carer has to be rewarded by that infant being responsive. The first relationship, which is the key to so much of our characters, is also the key to how something as abstract as a social system is internalized. The first experience of being in a relationship, which formats the way we experience later ones, also formats us to take the social system personally.

This is implied in E. P. Thompson's (1968) statement that 'class was not a thing but a relationship' and is made explicitly by Daniel Miller and Peter Jackson *et al.*(1998) when, in a study comparing two shopping centres, they describe the contrast between the centrepiece of the middle-class centre, a John Lewis department store, and the 'cheapjack stores' surrounding the more working-class one, as symbolizing a class difference which was internalized 'as a relationship within the individual', and used in the everyday processes of class and identity construction. It is big jump from how we read our mother's expression in early life, to how we experience class, but it is the prototype internalization. Being 'looked at' can be felt as loving, but it can also be felt as de-personalizing and as being stereotyped and, because visual interpretation is pre-verbal, it arouses very primitive feelings. Some evidence of this came out in the reactions to the Channel 4 programme 'Shops and Robbers', a television documentary about a woman who had made her living by shoplifting from Marks and Spencer, made for *Cutting Edge*. The programme had attracted an audience of 7.8 million viewers, the highest for the whole series.

Though screened some years before the interviews for this research took place, it was still well remembered, and perhaps because it was so shocking it often came up in discussion. Everyone who mentioned the film also mentioned how the woman 'wasn't at all how you'd expect a shoplifter to be', and how her performance as 'M&S woman' had been so convincing that she was hardly ever stopped, unlike the working-class shoppers discussing it, who were. They were shocked at the chutzpah of the woman, at how, 'She went to court in the morning and she was back out in the afternoon', and by the weak security of the store, 'Completely mad . . . I mean, exchanging goods without a receipt, amazing.' The film was unsettling for the middle-class viewers too, as it brought home to them the risk, almost routine for the working-class shopper, of being seen as a potential shoplifter, for the woman had been well dressed and looked just as they did.

The feelings and anxieties aroused by being 'looked at' in shops are possibly amplified by the ubiquitous mirrors and cameras, but they are also aroused because shopping, which offers us the opportunity to 'do' class, also exposes us to other people doing it too. It is not only women, or working-class people, who are subject to anxieties about how they are seen in shops. For example, one man from a lower-middle-class background, though now professionally very successful, described how he felt quite different leaving Marks and Spencer with a green or a white carrier bag (this was in the days when green bags denoted clothes, and white bags, food). The white carrier bag, he explained, 'said "Look, I can afford their food" you know, "I'm somebody with a busy life style, I like glamorous, slightly exotic foods, I'm a hip kind of person."' But he also wondered what he would say or feel if, when carrying a green bag, he met someone he knew who was 'really fashionable', since Marks and Spencer clothes signified something less classy and more staid than their food. Though Miller and Jackson *et al.* claim that Marks and Spencer 'did not seem to evoke a sense of class' (in contrast to Pollard and Adonis's firm placing of it as one of a small band of 'suppliers by appointment to the classless middle class') both the class position and the class messages given out by the store are complex. However, rather than cancelling class, the store serves as a mediating symbol of class. Famous for its success in selling 'knickers to the nation' and 'cashmere to the masses', the store appears to understand completely how different social groups use it. Some use it as a badge of being middle class, some use it to supply the occasional salve for the 'injuries of class', and some to disavow class. Whether these count as class strategies; the upper class are quite casual in their use of the store, the middle class see it more eye to eye, and expect it to be there for them, the lower middle class are more cautious, and the working class more ambivalent and fearful of being looked down upon. While the store's own class strategy is to play on the all-pervasive British consciousness of class. The food advertisements which start, 'This is not just a . . . whatever, it is an M&S . . . whatever', or even the 'Your M&S' campaign, which suggests all things to all people, implies that by buying M&S a person can be whatever class they want to be. If the dialectical method is to examine critically an issue from opposing positions, but always to assume that there is some common ground, then this is as good a description of the marketing strategy which launched the openly contradictory advertising campaigns of 'Exclusively for Everyone', or 'Making the Ordinary Extraordinary'.

A well-heeled academic once confided how he enjoyed shopping in Marks and Spencer because it allowed him to show, and feel, that he was 'just like other people'. Similarly, a very successful professional woman, acutely aware of how her clothes and position could evoke envy in colleagues, saw the store as providing her with clothes which could deflect or diffuse that envy because they 'said' 'You, too, can have this.' Another middle-class shopper saw the store as quite cleverly 'zonally targeted, with 'naffer acrylic sweater zones' and 'classier natural fibre zones', which were kept 'in designated areas appealing to certain classes', rather as men's and women's departments are kept separate. Another shopper, also middle class and much admiring of the store's skill in 'managing' class differences and its success in 'hanging on' to its 'loyal traditional clientele', described Marks and Spencer as having 'over-dubbed the potential leap-froggers' with 'a kind of sub-track which is slightly more colourful (and) has a kind of veneer of individuality to it'. Seeing his relationship to the store as 'a form of conversation', he told of how, having learned how to 'do' Marks and Spencer, he found 'a certain pleasure in having an opportunity to remind myself that I know how to do it . . . you know go to the men's clothes and know that there's no point in looking at the smart shirts that men wear with suits . . . and part of knowing how to do it is that although I wear ties a lot, I don't wear my ties with those shirts'. The man enjoyed knowing both how to follow and depart from dress codes, and he appreciated the store for having made it all 'so easy'. He also felt he knew what the store was up to, just as did the woman who was grateful for the 'naffer zones', which could be easily avoided.

Both shoppers showed an appreciation of the store as pleasantly attuned to them, and both appeared to expect that it would 'get it right' for them. This is part of the middle-class 'habitus', Pierre Bourdieu's (1977) term for the fit or attunement between a person and the place they are in. The middle classes in Britain typically take the store for granted, and even feel free to abuse it. An example is the middle-class shopper who claimed regularly to park her fretful children on sofas in the furniture department, while going off to explore on her own, just because she felt that she could. Or the man who claimed to have bought a suit from Marks and Spencer, worn it for one meeting, with the tag tucked in, and then returned it to the store. Even if the story was untrue, telling it involved no risk to the teller, as it would to a working-class man, and the raconteur did not think for one moment that he would be seen as dishonest. Treating shops proprietorially is both 'doing class' and 'showing off', and just as shops can 'call forth' the performance of gender, or the capacity to do mathematics, they can also call forth, at least from the middle-class shopper, the 'doing' of class as in behaving proprietorially and commenting upon other people. At a pinch some of the way shopping is used to 'do' class can be fitted into Bourdieu's (1977) general theory of culture, but his focus on 'embodiment', mainly as the result of hard physical work, and on 'practice', unvarying routine, does not fit well with the ultra flexible postmodern workplace, especially as many people do not work at all because they are on welfare. More relevant is Bourdieu's (1989) reply to the question put to him in an interview, of whether he thought classes existed, which was that 'there is always a space of difference where classes exist in a state of virtuality, not as something given, but as something to be done'. Shops can be seen both as spaces where classes exist in a state of virtuality, waiting to be done, and as spaces where class is done, in our heads, and by looking and being looked at. The self satisfaction which lies behind some 'basket snobbery' may not quite count as an exclusionary class strategy, but the woman in a supermarket queue remarking loudly to her husband about another family also shopping in the store, 'I thought that sort did their shopping at supermarket X', clearly wanted to be overheard by all nearby and, by drawing attention to herself, invited those people to join in her disapproval of this other family. Those others in the queue could nod in agreement, ignore her, or glance at each other with raised eyebrows, as most of us did, while checking our own ranking of supermarkets with hers. For myself, I could see little difference in the social status of the store where the woman thought the other family belonged, and where we were all standing. But small differences count a lot, and there could be no doubt that this woman saw the other family almost as trespassers, and would much have preferred that they shopped somewhere else.

Manners between people known to each other may have improved, and manners between staff and customers too, but the anonymity of shopping, plus its growth, and especially the growth of the supermarket, with its particular scopic possibilities, have created the conditions for class to continue to be 'done', if in a more patronizing and surreptitious way than in the past. There was nothing surreptitious about the woman who was grateful for the 'targeted zoning', and who was particularly pleased with how the store 'had its fingers on the pulse of fashions in food'. She singled out for particular praise a range of prepared salads which included 'nasturtium leaves and bits of borage blossom', which she found 'beautiful', 'absolutely up to the moment' and 'a really good thing, you know for the sort of poncier customers' as she self deprecatingly saw herself. She would probably not see those salads in the same way today, because that would no longer represent the store 'having its finger on the pulse'. However, the other side of the finger on the pulse is that items are deleted and, like many customers who take the store for granted, this woman regretted how often the store 'dropped things' just as she was beginning to like them. She gave as an example, 'the wonderful silk underwear . . . with very fine lace sewn into it' (and) the 'dark green tissues boxes with absolutely no horrible naffy designs on'. I am not suggesting that this woman would be anything other than genuinely courteous to whoever she met, and I quote her only to illustrate Cannadine's point about the British as always thinking about class and where they fit in and the 'individualistic turn'.

Standards of politeness are generally rather higher today inside shops than outside, and feeling a need, defensively, to 'put on a posh voice', is much less likely to be felt as necessary. This is, in part, because there are fewer independent stores, with idiosyncratic owners, and because of what is known in retail as the 'service revolution': the switch from competing on price to competing on the quality of the service offered to customers, the speedier transactions, easier returns policies, and staff trained less in knowledge of stock than in how to make customers 'feel good'. For example, staff in stores today are routinely taught 'never to point', and if asked by a customer for the location of some item, to drop whatever they are doing and immediately escort that customer to it, whoever he or she is. The shop assistant as 'friend' is more egalitarian than the older 'act' of the shop assistant as the 'servant'. This, plus the move towards hiring call-centre staff with more 'attractive' regional accents (attractive because they are less obviously class based), and younger staff in general, show a reduction in the overt symbolism of class and hierarchy. It is because standards of service in shops have improved that lapses such as the shop assistant who replied to Lynne Truss asking her about the price of an item missing its price tag with 'What do you think I am, psychic?', so shocked her that it drove Truss to write a book on modern manners. A kindred spirit is perhaps Alan Bennett (2005) nostalgically recalling how buying shoes used to involve,

> more what nowadays would be called interaction, the stock not laid out on racks for all to see and try on but secreted in banks of floor-to-ceiling boxes which were often accessible only on ladders, the assistants up and down them as nimble as sailors on the rigging. Customers, whatever their class, were deferentially treated ('Madame takes a broad fitting? Certainly'), and off they would go up the ladder again. It's a sign of my age that shoe shops seem nowadays to be staffed by sluts, indifferent, unhelpful and with none of that matronly dignity with which the selling of shoes and the buying of clothes were conducted. It is a small loss . . .

Perhaps Bennett was reacting to the absence of the more attentive service which is now taken for granted when shopping. Notwithstanding 'gated' malls shops, shopping districts and shopping centres are public civic spaces, and play a major part in making civil society civil and in helping to 'hold us together'.

Entitlement, respect and the 'public good'

The local pharmacy, post office or convenience store is every bit as critical as the doctor's surgery or police station for maintaining civil society and social cohesion. Retailers, who are obliged to co-operate with government over health and safety, planning and the collecting of taxes, often choose to co-operate further over other matters such as sharing the cost of surveillance cameras or, as in the London Borough of Waltham Forest, the 'community toilet scheme' where retailers make their lavatories available to the general public (the latter something of an irony since many former 'public conveniences' were closed by local authorities and the premises sold off to become small shops). Though there is no obligation on retailers to co-operate with government in the delivery of public services, other than over health and safety, the public–private divide has blurred and there are various schemes linking public services with shops. In the small Northumberland town of Hexham, a sign in the centre explains that the 'Police Community Beat Manager' will be in 'Tesco Extra, Alemouth Road, Between 1 p.m. and 3 p.m. every Thursday. Call in to discuss any policing issue. No appointment required.' Book stores encourage people not only to read books which they have not yet bought, but to read them alongside drinking coffee in the café, while cafés unattached to book stores encourage people to sit at tables with their laptops for hours without buying more than one coffee. This is done for business, but it is also used as a public service.

The communications potential of shops is part of what leads them to play this role, and a 'missing person' notice posted in a shop will be seen by many more people than the same notice in a police station, bus shelter or doctor's surgery. For the same reason, after a spate of particularly vicious murders of young women in Ipswich, Suffolk police mingled with Christmas shopping crowds to get across their safety messages. Shops are as much 'private' organizations as any other business, but 'free to enter' they boost a sense of entitlement. Hence the outcry in Britain following a government decision to support asylum seekers waiting for their cases to be heard by giving them not cash, but vouchers. The system was clearly a very poorly designed one, as the vouchers had to be obtained from a Post Office, and only some Post Offices kept them, which meant long journeys for the asylum seekers, much queuing, and often abuse from other customers inconvenienced by the sudden influx into 'their' Post Office. Once obtained, the vouchers were not widely accepted and the shops which did accept them often overcharged, did not sell the goods which the asylum seekers wanted, and had staff who no more understood the system than the asylum seekers (Eagle, Duff, Tah and Smith, 2002). This episode hit a nerve because it seemed to be almost a violation of a human right, and harked back to the 'truck' system when some factory owners shamelessly converted the already pitiful wages they paid workers into 'tokens' or 'scrips', which could only be 'spent' in shops owned by those same employers. The voucher system was not as bad as this, but it shocked a population not overly sympathetic to the plight of asylum seekers and, to make matters worse, after the system had been tried, found difficult to work, and then scrapped, it was tried again. This seemed almost to be the point, for the asylum seekers were not British citizens, or not yet, so appeared not to 'deserve' the freedom to shop where they wanted, for goods they wanted, at the same price as other people, and without being exploited, stigmatized or abused. Though the concept of relative deprivation has taken root, and the concept of need expanded beyond the physical to include social and psychological needs and an understanding of how possession of certain material goods, say a television or a car, are necessary for a person to be able to participate in civil society, there are still blanks in thinking around how those goods are accessed. The shame and stigmatization of the voucher was just as painful and demeaning for the asylum seekers as it had been for Jenny Diski when given a voucher, rather than money, to buy a pair of shoes, which also could not be bought in an ordinary shop. Only then there was no public outcry.

In the history of social progress, the right to shop, or to shop as others do, may not match winning the right to vote, belong to a trade union, or receive a living wage and support if unemployed, old or too sick to work. But shopping is a major form of 'participation' in modern society and the 'free-to-enter' shop is a potent social and political symbol of equality and the 'common culture'. State communism in Europe collapsed as much under the weight of consumer as political aspiration, and aspiration not just for cars other than Trabants, or lipstick in more than four colours, but also the satisfactions of shopping companionably in modern malls and plazas. The long queues and shortages of the communist era are not fondly remembered by those who can, and nor in Britain are the shrimp-pink spectacles which were once the only sort available 'on the NHS' (National Health Service). This is not to say that choice is all that citizens want, but points to the links between shopping, class and citizenship, and how ideas about rights and entitlements change. As living standards have risen, and populations come to expect them to continue to do so, political life has changed. The British Prime Minister Harold MacMillan went to the country in 1957 with the patronizing slogan 'You have never had it so good'. While in the United States, as Elisabeth Cohen (2003) details, the New Deal following the Second World War helped construct the 'citizen consumer' who expected rising living standards, and created what was virtually a 'consumer movement'.

The idea of citizenship is an evolving one and while it started with civil rights, justice and equality before the law, as T. H. Marshall (1950) showed, taking England as a case study, it gradually expanded to include political rights and, later, economic and social ones too. Each new set of rights laid the ground for further claims to be made and, taking this thesis further, Ralph Turner (1969) argued that a major theme of Western anti-discrimination movements during the twentieth century was that pride in being whoever you were was as important as not being discriminated against. This put respect as well as self respect, and even happiness, on the slate, moving those along similar tracks as poverty did a century earlier, from being seen as either a punishment or private misfortune, to a well recognized social and public issue (see Sennett 2003; Layard, 2005). The politics behind this development, the soaring costs of treatment, sickness absence, youth disaffection and crime on one hand, and rivalry among mental health care professionals on the other, are complex. But once happiness, self esteem and the refusal to tolerate disrespect have become policy issues, the question switches to what can be done? Shopping may not spring to mind as a possible solution, but the place where the satisfaction of being treated with respect has become an everyday right and where, for many people, happiness is found, is by going shopping. Though for some people just the thought of this is appalling, it can be helpful to consider the approach taken by Amartya Sen (1999) to human rights: that after secure access to adequate food, shelter, safety and clean water come a range of other conditions which, though harder to identify, are just as important for an individual 'to be the sort of person that they want to be, and live the sort of life that they have reason to value'. These conditions, of course, vary from culture to culture, but the notion of an 'ordinary' or 'normal' life, as one which we can take for granted, is important wherever we live and in the increasingly urbanized world shopping is part of that 'ordinary life' and shops are among the ordinary places where we can expect to be treated with respect.

Rescue and the ration book

The most compelling, if extreme, example of how shopping can foster social cohesion, is Britain during the Second World War or, as Angus Calder (1969) called it, 'The People's War', in which the rationing of food and other goods, along with the planned production of a limited number of luxury items (carrying the 'utility' mark), for consumption by the general population contributed, as Richard Titmuss (1958) showed, to the dramatic social changes in Britain in the twentieth century. The ration book and queue were both great levellers, and the temporary shops set up by the Women's Voluntary Service (WVS) to collect and distribute basic supplies, and help people get back to normal after bombing raids, led people from very different walks of life to co-operate. This was not always easy to achieve, as Nella Last's (1981) diaries record, but still it was achieved, in ways which would have been inconceivable before the war. 'Pulling together' was a major part of the 'war effort' and cheerful looking women, chatting and smiling while queuing outside shops were much photographed, giving a somewhat misleading impression since shopping during the war, with rationing and the black market, was very taxing (Sheridan, 1990). The photographs were essentially propaganda, as the British government had become acutely aware of the impact which shortages and queues had had on morale, on both the home and fighting fronts. The latter was especially true after a campaign to get women to write to their men in the services had backfired; far from the men being cheered up, they learned how difficult life was for their loved ones at home and for whom they were fighting (Jolly, 1997). From that point onwards the government, having commissioned regular 'Morale Reports' from Mass Observation, insisted that those reports included items on what was happening in the shops.

Among the changes of that time was that rationing established the practice of queuing in Britain, as you had to have your ration book stamped each time you used it; before this there had been more of a free-for-all in shops, as there is in a bar today. Though wartime also gave rise to a 'black market', a deeply divisive way of purchasing, the greater control assumed by government during the war allowed it to pass measures which in peacetime would have been more fraught. Introducing greater control over the distribution and quality of goods laid the ground for the public to develop more trust in shops, which had markedly not been the case for centuries (Benson and Ugolini, 2006). Trust, like respect, is necessary for citizenship to be meaningful and in Western societies today trust in shops often outdoes that of government or the Church, while in many parts of the world, drugs bought from shops are regarded as safer and superior to those available from state-run hospitals, even when the drugs obtained in that way are free (McKay, 2008). Not so long ago in Britain, something 'shop-made', which really meant 'shop bought', was seen as superior to a similar, but 'home-made', item. Arguably, branding has taken over from government as the guarantor of quality, a change from the time when the 'lion' stamp on an egg, a stamp issued by the 'Egg Marketing Board', had performed the trustworthy quality control role. Shops, just like products, are brands, and serve as benchmarks for quality too, as one friend illustrated when, to her chagrin, her cheesecake was judged by her father-in-law as 'almost as good as Marks and Spencer's'. In the United States it came as some surprise that it was

Wal-Mart which stepped in to help with the distribution of relief when the government emergency services were overwhelmed after hurricane Katrina devastated New Orleans in 2005.

On a different scale, after the Grand Hotel in Brighton was bombed by the IRA at the start of a Conservative Party Conference in 1984, the local Marks and Spencer store came to the rescue, even breaking the law about Sunday trading, and opened its doors so that delegates could quickly buy the wear they needed to continue with the conference. Marks and Spencer may be a special case, as part of its brand is to be seen as a national symbol, so it might be expected to step in at a moment of crisis. However, Wal-Mart was not such a symbol, or at least not in the same way. Crises are exceptional, of course, and larger operations have larger resources to offer. But in smaller ways smaller shops too come to the rescue, for example donating gifts to fairs held by local schools or to local charity events. This is good publicity, of course, but also it is expected. It is the expectation of rescue which makes shops important as cultural institutions and gets shopping 'under our skin' in such a way that it can be part of a larger holding operation. However, though trust in shops has grown, trust of shoppers has not and the rise of the store camera tells another story. This chapter has been about both the securities and insecurities produced and reproduced through and by shopping, and in part the next chapter continues with the theme of shops and security, but to conclude this one, it is worth remembering that, while every shop may be free to enter, not everyone feels equally free once inside.

7

Conclusion: Taking it all for Granted

'There's times when I just have to quit thinking . . . and the only way I can quit thinking is by shopping.'

Tammy Faye Bakker

In the introduction to this book I explained that one reason leading me to write it was the finding that, in the rich nations of the world, shopping was the activity on which, after work and sleep, we spent most time. It was a finding which raises the question of what, if we not buying goods when we go shopping, are we doing? As a result, a good part of the book has been an attempt to answer that question along the lines that shopping is both more and less than buying. It has also been to show that 'the more' and 'the less' add up to culture, and that this makes shopping a good lens through which to look at culture. I noted that because shopping is often marked down as a 'total waste of time', and we characteristically take shops and shopping for granted, the question becomes more whether we can see the meaning of what we are doing when we go shopping. So, for this conclusion, the question must be 'What did we see?' or, perhaps, 'What have we learned about culture which we did not know before?' To which the answer, for me, at least, is the impact of the unconscious.

In describing shopping as going in and out of our heads, as I did in Chapter 1, and the keeping of a shopping list at the back of our mind most of the day, I was indicating, more perhaps than, at first, I realized, the different levels of consciousness of shopping which are part of our everyday lives. In Chapter 2 I drew on Carol Gilligan's (2002) suggestion that there was a structural push towards 'dissociation' in the economic history of the West. This took the form of amnesia, which typically followed trauma for individuals. Gilligan applied the concept of dissociation to Western culture, which she saw as silencing a large chunk of women's experience. Whether through censorship or self censorship, women were driven 'not to know', or rather deny what they really knew. I used this to point up the dissociation which produces, on one hand, a discourse about shopping as all hedonism, irresponsibility, selfishness and extravagance, while at the same time the reality of shopping is clearly nothing like that ninety per cent of the time. The chapter tracked the consequences for women, and the reputation of shopping, following the trauma of the industrial revolution; the physical splitting of work from consumption that came with the breaking up of household production and housekeeping laid the foundation of the moral polarization of production and consumption and the people involved in those activities. And the chapter ended with a discussion of dissociation in the print media.

The place of shopping in unconscious processing is pretty clear in Chapter 3 on shopping memories and, as all memory is on the edge of consciousness, I suggested that what made shopping especially evocative, and thus memorable, was its narrative shape and way of disposing us to tell stories, which help us to fix or retrieve experience, and reproduce culture through the tool of narrative provided for us. I also started to make a case about shops as imaginative spaces which held the potential if not the promise of change. Chapter 4 on shopping through the life course was largely premised on the psychoanalytic account of human development of Erik Erikson (1950) and suggested that the same challenges and tasks which define our progression through life developmentally have parallels in the way we respond to and use shops, not always in very kindly ways. I also suggested that our relationship to shops, or the way we treat them, has something parent-like about it, and that we expect them to be 'attuned' to us, though, significantly, there is one section of the population, older people, to which the high street is most certainly not attuned. In Chapter 6 the idea that class relations had taken an 'individualistic turn' was used to explore how, in some contexts, shops could mediate class relations, but also how shops, especially the large supermarkets, provided scope for newer ways of 'doing' class which, in their effects on those to whom it was done, were every bit as effective as the old ways in terms of the unease produced.

In relation to culture understood as 'the arts', to point to unconscious processes playing a part is not a novel insight, as Freud (1910) made the case that all great art was the result of unconscious desires and drives being sublimated, and Melanie Klein (1930) saw art as reparation. When the debate about whether mass or popular culture was as worthy as 'high culture' was still a live one, popular culture tended to be regarded as inferior because, supposedly, it demanded less conscious effort, in contrast to high culture which demanded more. Shopping is more likely to be seen to belong with mass culture than 'high culture', with the exception of connoisseur-ship, which is not normally seen as shopping. The broader point, however, is that a hierarchy of mental functioning, which elevates cognition over affect, consciousness over unconsciousness, the 'finest minds' over 'inferior' ones, and the 'producers' of meaning over its 'consumers', is mapped on to social class. In his survey of writing about culture Terry Eagleton (2002) observes that consumers of popular culture have commonly been seen as more susceptible to unconscious processes and, perhaps, to being 'taken in' by advertising and he describes culture as 'a form of universal subjectivity at work within us', the 'the unconscious verso of the recto of civilized life'. Noting also that even T. S. Eliot, the high priest of high culture, acknowledged the role of the unconscious world when he wrote of that as 'the whole way of life of a people from birth to grave, morning to night, and even in sleep'.

Taken as a sample of culture, shopping is perhaps weighted towards the unconscious because of its connection with advertising, an industry which is widely thought to 'work' by planting associations and/or playing on insecurities in order to nudge the unknowing shopper towards whatever product the advertiser wants them to buy (see Mellencamp, 1992). But advertising has not been my concern, because this book has not been about buying particular goods, but about shopping as a process that is both more and less than buying. However, in every chapter, some reference has been made to unconscious meaning, or to some psychodynamic concept. The issue of psychological integration or re-integration, for either or both the individual and the community has come up in several chapters, but it is another step to suggest that the unconscious, or unconscious processing, forms a 'deep structure' which affects many of the meanings associated with shopping.

The concept 'deep structure' was proposed more than forty years ago by Noam Chomsky (1966) to capture the way grammar, which is the key to the meanings conveyed by language, seemed to be innate. Fascinated by how small children could use the rules of grammar without ever having been taught them, Chomsky reasoned that these rules were embedded in cognition as unconscious knowledge. The 'deep structure' which I am suggesting exists for shopping is not a cognitive unconscious, but a psychodynamic one. However, I am not suggesting that unconscious processes, or associations, account for all the meanings carried by or attributed to shopping, as meanings accrue from many directions. But we are all at the mercy of our inner worlds and these contain the imprints left by our early life experience, and in particular it is the traces of our first relationship, usually with our mother, which are critical. We do not remember this period, but that first relationship, internalized to form a working model, albeit an unconscious one, for how we think the world works, affects how we later approach the world and expect it to treat us (see Segal, 1991). Arguably, much of the joy some people find in shops and shopping, and the fear and loathing which others experience, are expressions of a more general capacity to find the world welcoming and generous, or withholding and punitive.

I am not suggesting that there is a grammar to shopping, though when in Chapter 1 I described shopping as 'punctuating' everyday life I was pointing to the way shopping can structure a day by breaking it up, and in that way give it meaning. Initially, I saw 'meaning', 'pattern' and 'structure' as the key words, but have come to see 'attachments' as equally significant and Attachment Theory, based on studies of how secure infants feel with their mothers, and how they respond to periods of separation from them, as giving another clue to the meanings made of shopping (see Holmes, 1993). The attachments established in early life, and the theory based on them, suggest that there are four main categories of 'attachment style': 'secure', 'insecure', 'ambivalent/ avoidant' and 'disorganized', and that this 'style' becomes permanent and shapes how subsequent relationships are approached and experienced. It is not hard to see possibilities for empirical research linking shopping style to attachment style, but it is not shopping patterns, but relationships with shops which are my concern, and I was drawn to Attachment Theory because it has been used to understand relationships with organizations (see Marris, 1991). As organizations, shops are very people-oriented, and they invite customers to build relationships with them, though ones which are not always quite what they seem, by using various incentives, loyalty cards, discounts, points schemes, singles evenings and, in the past, stamps.

But even without such incentives, if we look closely at the way many of us treat shops, taking them for granted, expecting them always to 'be there' for us, as and when we want them, and not thinking much about them in between times, we can see parallels with the parent or mother/child relationship. A place of safety, somewhere to turn to for comfort or respite, or to project anger; the shop is another version of the 'framed gap', Marion Milner's (1987) term for how the consulting room, bounded in time and space, but internally expansive and freeing, fosters or supports a re-integration of the self. Size and stability are both very evocative and they evoke qualities associated, at least ideally, with parents. The double standards which require adults/parents to be more patient, tolerant and better behaved than children, translate into the higher than average standards of courtesy expected of shop assistants than from customers, hence Lynne Truss's (2005) rage when they were not forthcoming. It was not just the offence of being spoken to so rudely, but shock at where it happened, in a shop, a context where a much more emollient, helpful and patient response was routine. The familialism which is part of what draws us to shops, also leads us to assume that we can freely explore their interiors and contents, whether or not we buy anything and, while openly rubbishing them, remain confident that they will patiently survive. The way we talk about loving or hating shopping is a further clue, as is the way we are often very cross and disappointed when we find shops unexpectedly shut, or discover that they do not have what we want. As infants we have to believe in the continued existence of our mothers and their capacity to give us what we want; and if we cannot, our very existence is thrown into doubt. Though no longer infants, the way we can seem personally affronted and throw a little tantrum shows we are in the grip of a state of mind which confuses the shop with a lived experience long ago. But this is less surprising when we consider how many levels there are on which the shop is equated with a person, indeed with a parent. In the US the term for the small general goods store is a 'mom and pop store', a name which, though it derives from the fact that there are no ex-family employees, nevertheless also carries the idea of the shop as 'the parents'.

However, the most obvious way experience of early life is mapped onto shopping is via feeding. Feeling comfortably well fed and generally confident that there will be food the next time it is wanted, or 'always hungry' and never sure about the next feed, and thus frantic about stocking up 'in case', is related to quite deep feelings of generalized anxiety and distrust that in the rich nations are rarely grounded in the real experience of hunger or serious shortage. The open doors of a shop may easily come to stand for the open and receiving arms of a mother and the hope that all will be made good within them. While the convention of treating the customer as 'always right' and, increasingly, 24/7 opening hours, so suggestive of feeding on demand, further invites us to develop expectations which are close to those an infant makes of its mother. Of course, shops are not our mothers, but if we treat them in a similar way it is because at an unconscious level some aspects of their 'offer' reiterates the time when 'greed' was good and 'eating up' was well rewarded. This is a fantasy, and far from being pathological is, as Julia Segal (1985) details, a major part of everyday life for all of us.

Infantile associations are further expressed by milk being the product most often bought from all-night stores, at least in Britain. We gossip about shops as we might people, commenting on what they have, what they look like, and how they have changed. Also, we personalize our relations with them by giving them affectionate nick-names, for example, 'Woollies' or 'Marks and Sparks' and, in turn, retailers work hard on building their side of the relationship with customers. Even when the shopping is not face-to-face, retailers still strive to make the customer feel known. The online bookseller, Amazon, addresses returning customers by their first name and, just before concluding a purchase will suggest further titles which they think we might like because they were bought by other people like us. If a good mother is the one who knows her child so well that it barely has to express a wish before it is met, then this is an attempt by Amazon to replicate that experience. Some of the most successful retailers are those who are especially 'attuned' to their customers, and for many years the chain store Marks and Spencer was so proud of how its customers told it 'what they wanted' that, prior to the crisis of 1998, it saw little need to advertise.

But the strongest evidence of attachment-style relations to shops lies in the reactions to their closure, and the departures of landmark shops are often an occasion for grief. For many Londoners, the departure of Jones Brothers from the Holloway Road, John Barnes from the Finchley Road, or Pratts from Streatham High Road, are still grieved over decades after they closed down. Ask for directions in the area around the Holloway Road from an older person, and to this day you are likely to be given them in terms of 'where Jones Brothers was', even though Jones Brothers has not been there for over thirty years. So it is with other landmark family stores in other cities. What is mourned when a shop closes is not only the shop, its convenience or quirkiness, but the way of life with which it was once bound up. Many older Britons today would still rather pay their gas and electricity bills at a shop, than by post or direct debit, because this is more personal and keeps alive a way of life which suits them, and, possibly, memories of a life shared with a partner. There are still more who, recently bereaved, embark on a shopping spree: sometimes for large items, such as new household equipment or a car, which the surviving spouse may have long wanted but feared, or knew, that their partner would have vetoed. The splurge may be felt partly as compensation for the loss, or as an extravagant protest against being made single and poor again, or as a sudden sense of freedom.

The connection to, and feeling for, particular shops, and the attempt to keep them alive by continuing to talk about them, is a further similarity with how we behave in human relationships. If there is a difference between grief following separation, or loss of a person we love and depend upon, and how we react to the closure of shops we have come to love, or depend upon, that difference is not obvious. Voices lower and fears are expressed about what will happen next to the site, the staff, and to the customer, for mixed up with the fate of the store are fears and feelings about customers' own futures too. This is partly a practical issue, of where and how they will, in future, find the goods which they had relied on that store to provide, and partly how near they are to their own demise. As the department store near where I live closed, speculation about the final sale was almost ghoulish. This is the point about attachment, it is an essential part of our humanity to seek and maintain relationships. If we mourn shops when they close, it is because the relationships we have built up with them have acquired what Robert Weiss (1991) calls 'attachment properties'. Weiss was not thinking of shops when he wrote this, but of relationships other than those between mothers and infants, or couples, but which had the depth to count as an 'attachment relationship', as do many friendships and work relationships. This fusion of feelings for shops as people was made abundantly clear when, after Marks and Spencer hit a bad patch just before the millennium, one of its first emergency measures was to close the overseas stores. In response, disappointed customers in Lille, France, opened a condolence book. And when the memorial service for Marcus Sieff, member of one of the founding families, was held just a day after a particularly dramatic fall in profits, it was described as 'in almost every way a memorial service for the old Marks and Spencer' (see Bevan, 2001: 240).

The (con)fusion or equation of shop with parent, which operates at several levels, both conscious and unconscious, might be expected as shopping and family life are also braided together at many layers. Shopping is a part of kinwork and is deeply embedded in family process, whether by provisioning the household or buying presents for relatives. We often talk possessively about shops, as in 'my' baker or butcher, when we could easily say 'the' baker or 'the' butcher. The familialism of shopping which enhances the sense of being in a relationship with a shop, is accentuated by many shops having started off as family businesses, and then keeping a family name as a way of keeping the family brand. With members of founding families being often well known, locally or nationally, businesses associated with families tend to carry a sense of being especially caring. The John Lewis Partnership, another iconic British retailer, though never as openly paternalistic as some family firms, trades on the claim that it is 'never knowingly undersold' and that its staff are also its partners and shareholders. Both the partnership and the promise not to 'knowingly undersell' suggest a business which has the 'best interests' of the 'customer/child' at heart, and, perhaps, is a 'good enough' parent.

The centrality of family relationships to shopping is the basis too of Daniel Miller's (1998) analysis of shopping as sacrifice. Impressed by the structural similarity between the shopping and sacrifice, both devotional and highly ritualized, it was made meaningful for the person performing the rite by serving to 'keep going' a relationship with the object of their devotion. In the case of sacrifice this will be a God, in the case of most ordinary shoppers, an ordinary husband, child, parent or sibling. But there is a further similarity, for both processes require the transformation of matter through some precise action. In our culture spending money on someone else is often a means of expressing love, and Miller shows how, within the careful budgeting of everyday shopping, what is also budgeted for is the odd 'treat'; occasionally this treat is for the self, but more usually it is for the 'devotional objects' and, most often, for a child. But even without the purchase of the particular pork pie, gherkin or seedless raspberry jam, the 'keeping going' of the relationship which underpins the practice, and gives shopping its meaning, is done by the 'keeping in mind' of a particular person every step of the way, rather like touching a prayer wheel, or keeping a photograph in the wallet or on a car sun visor. Thus, Miller concludes, shopping is 'the labour of constituting both the immediacy and the dynamics of specific relations of love'.

The web of associations, both conscious and unconscious linking shopping to women, or mothers, is part both of the 'deep structure', and the critique of shopping as selfish, irresponsible and a 'waste of time'. The gendered nature of shopping was discussed in Chapter 5, and in particular in relation to shops standing for the female body from which a man might want to flee, but not in relation to the 'deep structure' or unconscious which, as Freud saw it, 'knew no time' or, as Julia Kristeva (1981) put it, it is the experience of the womb which leads women to be equated with the point of origin, 'being', 'stasis' and timelessness, and men with time, action, doing and movement away. Time is ever a difficult concept to grapple with, but 'catching hold' of time is central to how a sense of self and personal autonomy develops. Paediatrician and psychoanalyst Donald Winnicott (1961) thought the infant could only 'catch hold of time' if its mother could herself be timeless and patiently wait for her child to finish a feed, stop crying or just get to sleep. An initial mutuality or feeling of being merged between mother and child becomes the basis for the infant's own sense of personal continuity. The point is that we are not born with a sense of time, but have to learn it, and do so, as with much else by 'taking it' from our mothers.

In conscious reality, women are every bit as time pressed as men, perhaps more so because their time is harder to protect, precisely because of the unconscious associations and the assumption, traceable to the fantasy of maternal omnipotence, that women can, and should, 'make time' for others, and which, as Doris Lessing (1994) complains, leads to very few people, 'perhaps one in fifty', being able to respect women's privacy. She continues that when she would say, 'I spend my mornings writing', this could not prevent the furtive knock on the door, and then a moment later, the guilty, embarrassed, smiling face appearing around the edge of the door, 'I've just dropped in for a *second*.' In the unconscious each sex is differently positioned to time, and this shows up in the way, stereotypically, each sex views shopping: men just wanting to 'get it done', as it is really a 'waste of time' and women, at least sometimes, finding shopping restorative and an escape into an 'oasis of timelessness', the same constant timelessness which they represent for others, but rarely find for themselves. Shops and shopping are not the only places, or activities, able to induce timelessness, and we often say that we 'don't know where time has gone', but shopping and shops have different paces, slow in the Post Office, fast at the newsstand outside a station, and sometimes the losing of time is exactly what is sought by going shopping. How we view and treat shops is obviously affected by our experience of them, both conscious and unconscious, and in this chapter I have explored some of the possible unconscious associations and meanings which we bring to shopping. It might be useful to compare the different ways in which we approach shops, which are fixtures, and fairs and markets which, while also fixtures, once a week or once a month, are not so fixed. Going to the fair, or market, is often experienced as more exciting and offering greater novelty than shops which are associated more with routine and predictability. The issue is not so much what the shops or markets are, but what they can represent; and if shops stand for safety, reliability and security the question is how might this affect their customers and, perhaps, encourage them to be more adventurous and creative? Although stock and layout may change, shops themselves do so less often, and our reaction, when they do change or close is often one of shock as, like our parents, we assume that shops are just there for us, like the little girl in Eudora Welty's (1979) story 'The Little Store', to use as we will.

References

Barber, Bernard (2007) *Consumed. How Markets Corrupt Children, Infantilise Adults and Swallow Citizens Whole*, New York, W. W. Norton.

Beck-Gernsheim, Elizabeth (1998) 'On the way to a post-familial family: from a community of need to elective affinities', in Mike Featherstone (ed.) *Love and Eroticism*, London, Sage.

Bell, Daniel (1976) *The Cultural Contradictions of Capitalism*, London, Heinemann.

Benjamin, Walter (1999) *The Arcades Project,* London, Belknap Press.

Berry, Neil (2008) *Articles of Faith,* London, Waywiser.

Bennett, Alan (2005) 'County arcade, Leeds', in *Untold Stories,* London, Faber and Faber.

Benson, John and Ugolini, Laura (eds) (2006) *Cultures of Selling: Perspectives on Consumption and Society Since 1700,* Aldershot, Ashgate.

Berger, Peter and Thomas Luckmann (1966) *The Social Construction of Reality,* London, Allen Lane, Penguin.

Bevan, Judy (2001) *The Rise and Fall of Marks and Spencer*, London, Profile Books.

Blythman, Joanna (2004) *Shopped: The Shocking Power of British Supermarkets*, London, Fourth Estate.

Bollas, Christopher (1992) *Being a Character: Psychoanalysis and Self-Experience,* London, Routledge.

Bourdieu, Pierre (1977) *Outline of a Theory of Practice,* Cambridge, Cambridge University Press.

— (1979) *Algeria 1960; The Disenchantment of the World; The Sense of Honour; The Kabyle House or the World Reversed,* Cambridge, Cambridge University Press.

— (1989) 'Social space and symbolic power', *Sociological Theory,* 7(1),: 14–25.

Bowden, Sue and Avner Offner (1996) 'The technological revolution that never was: gender, class and the diffusion of household appliances in interwar England', in Victoria de Grazia with Ellen Furlough (eds) *The Sex of Things. Gender and Consumption in Historical Perspective,* Berkeley, University of California Press.

Bowlby, Rachel (1985) *Just Looking: Consumer Culture in Dreiser, Gissing and Zola,* New York, Methuen.

Bruner, Jerome (1960) *The Process of Education,* New York, Vintage Books.

— (1987) 'Life as Narrative' *Social Research,* 54 (1).

— (1991) 'The Narrative Construction of Reality', *Critical Inquiry,* Autumn, 18: 1–21.

— (2002), *Making Stories: Law, Literature, Life,* Cambridge, Mass., Harvard University Press.

Calder, Angus (1969) *The People's War, Britain 1939–1945,* London, Jonathan Cape.

Campbell, Colin (1987) *The Romantic Ethic and the Spirit of Modern Consumerism.* Oxford, Blackwell.

— (1997) 'Shopping, pleasure and the sex war', in Pasi Falk and Campbell, Colin (eds) (1997)*The Shopping Experience,* London, Sage.

Cannadine, David (1998) *Class in Britain,* New Haven, Yale University Press.

Carrington, Christopher (2002) *No Place Like Home: Relationships and Family Life among Lesbians and Gay Men,* Chicago, University of Chicago Press.

Chomsky, Noam (1966) *Cartesian Linguistics: A Chapter in The History of Rationalist Thought,* London, Harper.

Clark, Alan (1993) *Diaries: In Power 1983–1992 vol. 1,* London, Weidenfeld and Nicolson.

Cohen, Elisabeth (2003), *A Consumer's Republic. The Politics of Mass Consumption in Post War America*, New York, Knopf.

Cohen, Stanley and Laurie Taylor (1976) *Escape Attempts. The Theory and Practice of Resistance to Everyday Life*, London, Allen Lane.

Craib, Ian (1994) *The Importance of Disappointment*, London, Routledge.

Crane, Diana (2000) *Fashion and its Social Agendas. Class, Gender, and Identity in Clothing*, Chicago, University of Chicago Press.

Cunningham, Michael (2000) *The Hours*, London, Fourth Estate.

Davidson, James, N. (1998) *Courtesans and Fishcakes: The Consuming Passions of Classical Athens*, London, Fontana Press.

de Certeau, Michael (1988) *The Practice of Everyday Life*, Berkeley, University of California Press.

De Vault, Marjorie (1994) *Feeding the Family: The Social Organization of Caring as Gendered Work*, Chicago, University of Chicago.

Diski, Jenny, (2002) 'Diary' *London Review of Books*, 14.11.2002.

Douglas, Mary (1997) 'In defence of shopping', in Pasi Falk and Colin Campbell (eds) *The Shopping Experience*, London, Sage,

Du Gay, Paul (1996) *Consumption and Identity at Work*, London, Sage.

Dunne, Gillian (1997) *Lesbian Lifestyles: Women's Work and the Politics of Sexuality*, Basingstoke, Macmillan.

Eagle, Andrea, Duff, Lesley, Tah, Carolyne, and Smith, Nicola (2002)*Asylum Seeker's Experience of the Voucher Scheme in the UK: Fieldwork Report,* Home Office Research, Development and Statistics Directorate. March 2002.

Eagleton, Terry (2002) *Culture*, Oxford, Blackwell.

Ehrenreich, Barbara (2001) *Nickel and Dimed: On (Not) Getting By in America*, New York, Henry Holt.

— (1990) *Fear of Falling the Inner Life of the Middle Class,* New York, Harper Collins.

Erikson, Erik H. (1950) *Childhood and Society*, New York, W. W.Norton and Co.

Felski, Rita (2002), 'The invention of everyday life', *New Formations* (39): 15–31.

Fox, Kate (2004) *Watching the English. The Hidden Rules of English Behaviour*, London, Hodder and Stoughton.

Freud, Sigmund (1901) 'Childhood memories and screen memories', in *The Psychopathology of Everyday Life,* Pelican Freud Library, Harmondsworth, Penguin.

Freud, Anna (1969) 'About losing and being lost', in *Indications for Child Analysis and Other Papers 1945–1956*, London, The Hogarth Press.

Fry, Stephen, (1997) *Moab is my Washpot,* London, Hutchinson.

Gabriel, Yiannis and Lang, Tim (1995) The *Unmanageable Consumer. Contemporary Consumption and its Fragmentation*, London, Sage.

Galbraith, John Kenneth (1958) *The Affluent Society*, London, Hamish Hamilton.

Garfinkel, Harold (1969) *Studies in Ethnomethodology*, Englewood Cliffs, Prentice Hall.

— (1967) *Studies in Ethnomethodology*, Englewood Cliffs, New Jersey, Prentice Hall.

Gershuny, Jonathan (2002) *Changing Times. Work and Leisure in Post Industrial Society*, Oxford, Oxford University Press.

Gilligan Carol (2002) *The Birth of Pleasure,* New York, Alfred A. Knopf.

Goffman. Erving (1969) *The Presentation of Self in Everyday Life*, London, Allen Lane.

Gordon, Mary (2006) 'Now I am married', in *Temporary Shelter*, London, Penguin.

Gouldner, Alvin (1973) *For Sociology. Renewal and Critique in Sociology Today*, London, Allen Lane.

Grant, Linda (1998) *Remind Me Who I Am, Again*, London, Granta.

Hilton, Matthew (2003) *Consumerism in 20th-Century Britain*, Cambridge, Cambridge University Press.

Hine, Thomas (2002) *I Want That: How We All Became Shoppers. A Cultural History*, New York, HarperCollins.

Hofstede, Geert (1998) 'Masculinity/femininity as a dimension of culture', in Geert Hofstede *et al.*(eds) *Masculinity and Femininity. The Taboo Dimension of National Cultures*, Sage, Thousand Oaks.

Holmes, Janet (1998) 'Complimenting – a positive politeness strategy', in Jennifer Coates (ed.) *Language and Gender: A Reader,* Oxford, Blackwell.

Holmes, Jeremy (1993) *John Bowlby and Attachment Theory*, London, Routledge.

Horowitz, Daniel (1985) *The Morality of Spending*, Baltimore, The Johns Hopkins University Press.

Horrell, Sara and Jane Humphries (1995) 'Women's labour force participation and the transition to the male-breadwinner family, 1790–1865', *Economic History Review*, 48, 1: 89–117.

Hughes, Kathryn (2005) *The Short Life and Long Times of Mrs Beeton*, London, Fourth Estate.

Humphries, Jane (1977) 'Class struggle and the persistence of the working class family', *Cambridge Review of Economics,* 1: 241–58.

Hutton, Will (2002) *The World We Are In*, Little, Brown, London.

James, Oliver (2007) *Affluenza: How to Be Successful and Stay Sane,* London, Vermillion.

James, Oliver (2006) 'Workaholic consumerism is now a treadmill and a curse' *Guardian*, 2 February 2006.

Jacques, Martin (2004) 'The death of intimacy', *Guardian,* 18 September 2004.

Jeffery, T. (1999) *Mass Observation: A Short History*. M-OA Occasional Paper No. 10, University of Sussex Library, Mass Observation Archive, University of Sussex Library.

Jolly, Margaretta (1997) 'Everyday letters and literary form: correspondence from the Second World War', D.Phil. thesis. University of Sussex.

Klein, Naomi (2000) *No Logo*, London, HarperCollins.

Kristeva, Julia (1981) 'Women's Time', *Signs*, 7.

Lakoff, George and Johnson, Mark (1980) *Metaphors We Live By*, Chicago, University of Chicago.

Latour, Bruno (2005), *Reassembling the Social: An Introduction to Actor-Network Theory*, Oxford, Oxford University Press.

Last, Nella (1981) *Nella Last's War: A Mother's Diary,1939–1945,* Bristol, Falling Wall Press.

Lave, Jean (1988) *Cognition in Practice: Mind, Mathematics and Culture in Everyday Life*, Cambridge, Cambridge University Press.

—(1996) 'The practice of learning', in Seth Chaiklin and Jean Lave (eds) *Understanding Practice: Perspectives on Activity and Context*, Cambridge, Cambridge University Press.

Lawson, Neal (2006) 'Turbo-consumerism is the driving force behind crime', *Guardian,* 29 June 2006

— (2009) *All Consuming: How Shopping Got Us Into This Mess and How We Can Find Our Way Out*, London, Penguin.

Layard, Richard (2005) *Happiness: Lessons from a New Science*, London, Allen Lane.

Lessing, Doris (1994) *Under My Skin. Volume One of My Autobiography, to 1949,* London, Harper Collins.

Levine, Judith (2006) *Not Buying It. My Year Without Shopping,* New York, Simon and Schuster.

Lofgren, Orvar (1988) 'My life as a consumer: narratives from the world of goods', in Mary Chamberlain and Paul Thompson (eds), *Narrative and Genre,* London, Routledge.

Peter Marris (1991) 'The social construction of uncertainty', in Colin Murray Parkes, Joan Stevenson-Hinde and Peter Marris (eds) *Attachment Across the Life Cycle,* London, Routledge.

Marshall, T. H. (1950) *Citizenship and Social Class, and Other Essays,* Cambridge, Cambridge University Press.

MacIntyre, Alistair (1981) *After Virtue: A Study in Moral Theory,* London, Duckworth.

Mckay, Bruce (2008), 'From life insurance to safer sex: reflections of a marketing man', *Social Science and Medicine,* 66: 2168–72.

Mellencamp, P. (1992) *High Anxiety: Catastrophe, Scandal, Age and Comedy,* Bloomington, Indiana University Press.

Menzies-Lyth, Isabel (1989) 'The purchase and consumption of chocolate', in *The Dynamics of the Social. Selected Essays,* London, Free Association Books.

Mikel Brown, Lynne, and Gilligan, Carol (1992) *Meeting at the Crossroads: Women's Psychology and Girls' Development,* Cambridge, Harvard University Press.

Miller, Daniel (1998) *Theory of Shopping,* Cambridge, Polity.

Miller, Daniel, Jackson, Peter and Thrift, Nigel, with Holbrook, Beverley (1998) *Shopping, Place and Identity,* London, Routledge.

Miller, Daniel and Fiona Parrott (2009) 'Loss and material culture in South London', *Journal of the Royal Anthropological Institute,* 15(3): 502–19.

Miller, Geoffrey (2009) *Spent,* Viking Books, London.

Milner, Marion (1987) 'The framed gap', in *The Suppressed Madness of Sane Men. Forty Years of Exploring Psychoanalysis,* Tavistock, London.

Monbiot, George (2007) 'For the sake of the world's poor we must keep the wealthy at home', *Guardian,* 28 February 2006.

Nicolaas, G. (1995) *Cooking: Attitudes and Behaviour,* London, OPCS Social Survey Division.

Observer Newspaper (2004) 'Men Uncovered' Special Report.

Oz, Amos (2005) *A Tale of Love and Darkness,* London, Chatto and Windus.

Pahl, Janet (1989) *Money and Marriage,* Basingstoke, Macmillan.

Parkin, Frank (1979), *Marxism and Class Theory: A Bourgeois Critique,* London, Tavistock.

Patchett, Ann (1998) *The Magician's Assistant,* London, Fourth Estate.

Pollard, Stephen and Adonis, Andrew (1997) *A Class Act: The Myth of Britain's Classless Society,* London, Hamish Hamilton.

Roth, Philip (2006) *Everyman,* New York, Houghton Mifflin.

Ryan, Alan (1998) 'The Growth of a Global Culture', in Michael Howard and Wm Roger Louis (eds) *The Oxford History of the Twentieth Century,* Oxford, Oxford University Press.

Rybczynski, Witold (1991) *Waiting for the Weekend,* New York, Viking Penguin.

Saunders, Peter (1982) 'Beyond housing classes: the sociological significance of private property rights in means of consumption', University of Sussex, Urban and Regional Studies Working Papers. No. 33.

Saunders, Peter (1990) *A Nation of Home Owners,* London, Unwin Hyman.

Schama, Simon (2004) *The Embarrassment of Riches: An Interpretation of Culture in the Golden Age,* London, Fontana Press,

Scheff, Thomas (1984) *Being Mentally Ill. A Sociological Theory.* New York, Aldine.

Schor, Juliet (2004) *Born to Buy: The Commercialized Child and the New Consumer Culture,* London, Scribner.

Scitovsky, Tibor (1986) *Human Desire and Economic Satisfaction: Essays on the Frontiers of Economics,* Brighton, Wheatsheaf Books.

Segal, Julia (1991)*Phantasy in everyday life: a psychoanalytical approach to understanding ourselves,* London, Penguin.

Seiter, Ellen (1995) *Sold Separately: Children and Parents in Consumer Culture,* New Brunswick, NJ, Rutgers University Press.

Sen, Armartya (1999) *Commodities and Capabilities,* Amsterdam, North Holland.

Sennett, Richard (2003) *Respect the Formation of Character in a World of Inequality,* London, Allen Lane.

Shaw, Jenny, (1998) 'Feeling a list coming on: gender and the pace of life', *Time and Society,* 7 (2): 383–96.

Sheridan, Dorothy (ed.) (1990) *Wartime Women: A Mass-Observation Anthology 1937–45,* London, Heinemann.

— (1993) 'Ordinary hardworking folk?': volunteer writers for Mass Observation 1937–50 and 1981–91, in *Feminist Praxis,* 37/8.

— (1996) 'Damned anecdotes and dangerous confabulations'. *Mass Observation as Life History,* M-OA Occasional Paper No. 7, University of Sussex Library.

Simms, Andrew (2007) *Tescopoly. How one shop came out on top and why it matters,* London, Constable and Robinson.

Smelser, Neil, J. (1959) *Social Change in the Industrial Revolution: An Application of Theory to the Lancashire Cotton Industry, 1770–1840,* London, Routledge.

Stewart, Susan (1984) *On Longing: Narratives of the Miniature, the Gigantic, the Souvenir, the Collection,* Baltimore, Johns Hopkins.

Taylor, Ian (1999) *Crime in Context: A Critical Criminology of Market Societies,* Cambridge, Polity.

Thompson, E. P. (1963) *The Making of the English Working Class,* London, Pelican Books.

Thompson, Paul (1990) *I Don't Feel Old: The Experience of Older Life,* Oxford, Oxford University Press.

Tilly, Charles (2006) *Why? What Happens When People Give Reasons . . . and Why,* Princeton, Princeton University Press.

Titmuss, Richard (1958) 'War and social change', in *Essays on the Welfare State 1907–1973,* London, Allen and Unwin.

Truss, Lynne (2005) *Talk to the Hand: The Utter Bloody Rudeness of Everyday Life,* London, Profile Books.

Turner, Ralph (1969) 'The theme of contemporary social movements', *British Journal of Sociology,* 20(4): 390–405.

Turner, Victor (1970), *The Forest of Symbols: Aspects of Ndembu Ritual,* New York, Cornell University Press.

Underhill, Paco (1999 or 2000) *Why We Buy: The Science of Shopping,* New York, Simon and Schuster.

Vickery, Amanda (1998) *The Gentleman's Daughter: Women's Lives in Georgian England,* New Haven, Yale University Press.

Waddell, Margot (2002) *Inside Lives, Psychoanalysis and the Growth of the Personality,* London, Karnac Books.

Watts, Jonathan (2006) 'Invisible city', *Guardian,* 15 March, 2006.

Weber, Max (1930) *The Protestant Ethic and the Spirit of Capitalism,* London, Allen and Unwin.

Weiss, Robert (1991) 'The attachment bond in childhood and adulthood', in Colin Murray Parkes, Joan Stevenson-Hinde and Peter Marris (eds) *Attachment Across the Life Cycle,* London, New York, Routledge.

Welch, Evelyn (2005) *Shopping in the Renaissance,* Newhaven and London, Yale University Press.

Welty, Eudora (1979) 'The little store', in *The Eye of the Story: Selected Essays and Reviews,* New York, Random House.

West, Candace and Zimmerman, Don (1987) 'Doing Gender', *Gender and Society,* 1 (2): 125–51.

Williams, Raymond, (1958) 'Culture is ordinary', in Norman Mackenzie (ed.) *Convictions,* London, MacGibbon and Kee. Reprinted in Williams, Raymond (1989) *Resources of Hope,* London, Verso.

— (1976) *Keywords,* London, Fontana Publications.

Williams, Rosalind (1982) *Dream Worlds,* Berkeley, University of California Press.

Winch, Peter (1958) *The Idea of a Social Science and its Relation to Philosophy,* London, Routledge.

Winnicott, Donald (1961) 'Notes on the time factor in treatment', in R. Shepherd, J. Johns and H. Taylor Robinson (eds), *Winnicott and Thinking about Children,* London, Karnac Books.

— (1967) 'Mirror-role of mother and family in child development', in *Playing and Reality,* London, Tavistock.

— (1971) 'Playing: its theoretical status in the clinical situation', in *Playing and Reality,* London, Tavistock.

Woodward, Kathleen (1991) *Aging and its Discontents, Freud and Other Fictions,* Bloomington, Indiana University Press.

Woolf, Virginia (1925) *Mrs Dalloway,* London, The Hogarth Press.

Wright Kenneth (1991) *Vision and Separation: Between Mother and Baby,* London, Free Association Books.

Younge, Gary (2007) 'Comment-debate' *Guardian,* 13 August 2007.

Zerubavel (1989) *The Seven Day Circle: The History and Meaning of the Week,* Chicago, University of Chicago Press.

Zukin, Sharon (2004) *Point of Purchase. How Shopping Changed American Culture,* New York, Routledge.

Index